Isaac Mayer Wise

The cosmic God, a Fundamental Philosophy in Popular Lectures

Isaac Mayer Wise

The cosmic God, a Fundamental Philosophy in Popular Lectures

ISBN/EAN: 9783743393325

Manufactured in Europe, USA, Canada, Australia, Japa

Cover: Foto ©Lupo / pixelio.de

Manufactured and distributed by brebook publishing software (www.brebook.com)

Isaac Mayer Wise

The cosmic God, a Fundamental Philosophy in Popular Lectures

PREFACE.

This book, conceived in sorrow, composed in grief, and constructed at the brink of despair, contains my mind's best thoughts, and my soul's triumph over the powers of darkness. My wife, my dearly beloved companion in this eventful life, the mother of my childdren, the faithful partner of my joys and my sufferings, was prostrated 'with an incurable disease. For nearly two years she lived the life of a shadow, without affection or clear consciousness, no more herself than the ruin is the castle. I prayed, I wept, I mourned, I despaired; and yet my cup of woe was not full. A feeling which I can not describe, in clashing conflict with the above, against which my sense of duty rebelled, and my better nature continually and forcibly remonstrated, overwhelmed me so irresistably, with such inexpressible violence, that I was drifting and whirling about in a roaring current of lacerating contradictions, tormenting self-accusations bordering on self contempt.

Ruthless attacks upon my character, of restless assailants, from the camp of implacable foes, embittered my joyless days. My energies failed. Insanity or suicide appeared inevitable. In this state of mind, the Satan of Doubt persecuted me with all his furious demons. My convictions were uprooted, and my faith was shaken; I was myself no longer. Once, at the midnight hour, in a state of indifference and stupor, I opened the Bible, and perchance I read:

"Unless thy law had been my delights, I should long since have been lost in my affliction." (Psalms 119, 92.)

It struck me forcibly: "There is the proper remedy for all afflictions." When those ancient Hebrews spoke of the law of God, they meant the whole of it revealed in God's words and works. Research, science, philosopy, deep and perplexing, problems most intricate and propositions most complicated, I thought, like the rabbis of the talmud, must be the proper remedy for all maladies of the heart and reason. I plunged headlong into the whirlpool of philosophy, and, I believe, to have found many a gem in the fathomless deep. But the costliest of all gems I found is a calm and composed mind, a self-relying conviction. I found myself once more. My sainted wife having been the first cause of this turn in my life's history, and this volume containing the first fruits of my independent researches in science and philosophy, I have dedicated it to her memory.

I had lectured every Friday evening for two successive winters on the History of Philosophy, with special reference to the Jewish philosophers down to Baruch Spinoza and Moses Mendelssohn, and published sketches thereof in *The Israelite*. Meanwhile I read the modern books on philosophy and science, especially by German authors. In the summer of the year 1874, under the most distressing circumstances, I sketched the course of lectures now laid before the public, and delivered them in the fall and winter of 1874-5, in the Temple of the Benai Yeshurun Congregation of Cincinnati, and published extensive abstracts thereof in *The American Israelite*. The Cincinnati daily papers, especially the *Enquirer*, and my audience encouraged me so kindly, that I revised those lectures to give them to the public in the present form, as a genuinely American production of the philosophizing mind.

No metaphysics! No transcendant and no transcendental philosophy! No formal speculations!—the good natured, sweet tempered and self-complacent pastor exclaims, blessed either with a superabundance of uninquired faith, or with the consciousness of his inability to confront the spirit of the age with its new problems, forced upon the thinking mind by the successes and discoveries of science, and advertised in a variety of forms by a class of so called free thinkers, whose voice reaches all classes of society, down to the village school-room. The days of touching simplicity are gone, This is an age of sober reflection, deep and irresistable. Either you are able of defending your dogmas before the judgment seat of reason, or you must see them antiquated and impotent. The conflict of science and religion is before your doors, however sentimentally and devotionally you may whitewash the crumbling walls, or galvanize defunct forms, or close your eyes in fervent prayer, to see not how the platform shakes under your feet. You must defend yourselves or surrender. What are your arms of defence, if you philosophize not?

Again, the scientist, and the specialist in particular, who attempts to coustruct the universe in compliance to the laws governing one science, is no less opposed to philosoyhy than the sentimental pastor. It is natural that the scientist, engaged in investigating empirically isolated phenomena, classifying formally the analogous facts, and seeking by experience and experiment the law which governs them respectively, should be so engulfed in empiricism and one-sided particularism that the universe appear to him submerged in his particular science, beyond which there is nothing. But philosophy is not a merely systematical cognition of a class of things or even all things ; it is the cognition of the principles, the summation and harmonization of the deepest relations of all physical and spiritual essence; it is the first and also the last of all sciences, from which all of them emerged, and in which all of them finally submerge. The sciences are the building stones of philosophy, from which it construes the system of the universe, in which all is in its proper place, and all parts are united to a harmonious totality. Philosophy extends beyond each science and all sciences, as far as intelligence reaches beyond phenomenal nature. The systems of philosophy must be different on account of the different philosophizing subjects, the various starting points, and the scientific means at the command of each; but the object of philosophy is invariably the same, and each of the systems has contributed its share to the solution of the gigantic problem, What is this universe?

In the volume before you, I have made the attempt to respond to this question. Reviewing the sciences in connection with the main points of the problem, adhering strictly to the law of causality and the method of induction, I believe to have reached a definite conception of the universe, and the God of the universe. Therefore I consider this a fundamental philosophy, from which the various philosophical disciplines can be derived. The universe, with the exception of matter, which is a very small fraction thereof, appearing to me synonymous with Deity, so that the present volume is in the main a new evidence of the existence of Deity, I have called it The Cosmic God, in whom and by whom there is the one grand harmonious system of things, in whom and by whom nature is a cosmos and no chaos.

I know well that this is not the God of vulgar theology, nor is it the God of Spinoza or Locke. I could not discover either of them in my researches into the phenomenal sciences and history. Theologians can give us no definition of Deity; their ideas are indefinite and vague, and consequently the cause of atheism. The God of Spinoza and Locke is submerged in nature, so that nature is God, and God is nature, beyond which there is nothing. The infinite has become finite in nature, and all is necessity. This excludes all principles of freedom and ethics. This pantheism, falsely called so, because the universe is infinitely more than all objects of nature, in the minds of dependent thinkers, changed into fatalism and materialism, lasts heavily upon the present generation. I did not arrive at either of those conclusions concerning Deity, simply because as free as possible from all prejudices, and from the present state of the sciences, I could reach THE COSMIC GOD only. If it is not the God of modern theology, He is God after all, the Eternal Jehovah, who will be worshiped by future generations.

THE AUTHOR.

CONTENTS.

Lecture.		Page.
I.	Truth and its Criterion,	9
II.	The Mind's Receptivity and Spontaneity,	16
III.	Mind or Brain,	23
IV.	Human Mind actualized in its Monuments,	32
V.	Second Lecture on same subject,	39
VI.	Homo-Brutalism Reviewed,	47
VII.	Homo-Brutalism—Reviewed Anatomically,	55
VIII.	Homo-Brutalism–Reviewed Psychologically,	62
IX.	Elementary Ontology,	70
X.	History of Materialism,	77
XI.	Dynamic Ontology,	85
XII.	Biology,	93
XIII.	Biology—Part II,	101
XIV.	Origin of Species,	108
XV.	Teleology,	119
XVI.	Will and Intellect in Nature,	127
XVII.	Superhuman Will and Intellect in History,	133
XVIII.	Superhuman Will and Intellect in History, —Concluded,	141
XIX.	Metaphysics.—I. God in Nature.	149
XX.	Metaphysics.—II. Nature's God.	157
XXI.	Nature and its Relation to Deity.	165
XXII.	Man in his Relations to God and Nature.	173

THE
COSMIC GOD.

A FUNDAMENTAL PHILOSOPHY IN

POPULAR LECTURES.

LECTURE I.

TRUTH AND ITS CRITERION.

LADIES AND GENTLEMEN—The object of the course of lectures to which this is introductory is to find truth by the instrumentality of inductive philosophy. It is now supposed that Hamlet was right in saying—

> "If circumstances lead me, I will find
> Where truth is hid, though it were hid indeed
> Within the center."

It is proposed to go over the whole ground of the philosophical problems which concern religion, in order to ascertain, after a fair and full consideration of the philosophy and the sciences of the nineteenth century, what remains to be held up as the religious doctrine of honest and intelligent people, without conflict with the intelligence of this enlightened and progressive age; what remains to be constructed into the religion of the future generation. Whatever philosophy and science have overcome, is dead, and the dead decays by its own inherent law. The corpse may be embalmed, but then it is a mummy. It is proposed to ascertain the living elements of truth. Therefore the first problem to be solved is, What is truth, and which is its criterion?

"What mark does truth, what bright distinction bear?
How do we know that what we know is true?
How shall we falsehood fly and truth pursue?"

What is truth? Facts and objects in themselves are neither true nor false; they are. Their representations in the human mind, the ideas, may be true and false. An idea is true if it is an accurate and complete mental image of the fact or object, or any of its parts or attributes which it represents. A negation is true if it denies that which exists not. But in all instances ideas only are true or false; facts and objects are neither.

The accurate, complete, and harmonious knowledge of all facts and objects is truth. The Omniscient only is in possession of absolute truth. In man, with whom knowledge is necessarily limited, truth is relative to his knowledge. In man, truth is the accuracy, completeness, and harmony of the facts and objects of his cognition. As long as one has no accurate and complete knowledge of the elements of his cognition, their aggregate must be defective; it is not truth. Analysis is reason's start in search of truth. If the elements of cognition are accurate and complete in the judgment of the thinking agent—but they are disharmonious, bearing in themselves the germs of contradiction—then their aggregate is not truth. The want of harmony in the cognitions proves their inaccuracy or incompleteness. Truth is synthetical. It is the unison in man's cognition and cognitions. You see all truth is ideal. Take away self-conscious intelligence, and there is no truth.

Harmony in the elements of our knowledge is the criterion of truth. There is no other. Therefore, in order to be sure that what we know is true, we must in the first place analyze the elements of our knowledge; and where this is possible, compare each image in the mind to its respective realty, within or without, to be convinced of their identity, and then control each idea by the necessary harmony among all of them.

Let us illustrate. Every person of sound mind and sense has some ideas of the shape, bulk, and distance of the sun. With persons who have no astronomical knowledge, these ideas are usually false, although they have observed the sun all the days of their lives, and are quite sure of their sensations, impressions, and perceptions; because they have never compared their ideas with the corresponding realities. Science has discovered the means to do this, and has established the spherical form of the sun, with a diameter of 850,100 miles, 107 times the mean diameter of the earth; with a bulk 600 times as large as that of all known planets together; and with a mean distance from the earth about 90,000,000 of miles. By comparison of idea and reality their identity was established.

Now suppose that a person ignorant of astronomy be told all these facts and numbers, their correlatives, and the scientific process by which they were established, his knowledge of the sun would still be incomplete, because he is ignorant of the mechanical and physical constitution of that luminary, as spectrum analysis and solar photography have revealed it. But knowing all this, he finds in his mind the idea of the sun moving around the earth, which he supposes to have observed repeatedly and clearly. Next he finds in his mind the idea that the larger body attracts the smaller, and that the motion of the sun or earth depends on the bulk of matter constituting them respectively. His ideas are in disharmony, and he knows at once that he is not in possession of truth. His cognitions require correction, until they are harmonized, and then only he has arrived at the truth of the matter. All cognitions of the individual thus harmonized with the cognitions of man universally, it is in possession of truth, as far as attainable at this stage of history.

This illustration proves not only man's innate abilities of correct comparison and judgment, which none doubts who admits the exactness of mathematics, but also that he possesses knowledge which has not reached him through the avenues of his senses, neither by any one, nor all of them in co-operation. All known facts concerning the solar system are contrary to the impressions which those bodies make on our senses. Therefore we take here for granted that man's knowledge originates but partly from the impressions received through his senses, while it orginates partly from some other scource. We call this other scource mind, spirit, or soul, with its feelings, volitions, and intelligence. Let us call these two elements in our knowledge, in relation to their origin, the sensual and the mental. Man has sensual knowledge of what he perceives by his senses and mental knowledge of what he brings forth by the exercise of his mind. To remain within the limits of our illustration, we would say he knows the sun, planets, and moons by sensual tuition; but he knows their shapes, bulks, distances, constitutions, rotations, and relations by mental cognition.

This illustration proves furthermore, that mental cognition is superior to sensual intuition and must control it. Had the mind not corrected the perceptions of the senses, the sun would still appear to us, as to all the animals, a flat circular section, forty or fifty feet in diameter, and a few thousand yards above our heads. This is a stumbling block to gross realism, for all do and must believe verities which they can neither see, hear, smell, taste or touch, and none can deny the exactness of mathematics. It is no less a stumbling block to scientific realism. While you listen to what I say, you receive by the sensual organ a knowledge of words, of successive articulate sounds, and no more; by your mind you grasp the knowledge of connected and consecutive thoughts, propositions, arguments, evidence, and conclusions which stand in no imaginable relation to the air's motion caused by my speaking, as little, indeed, as the mere sight of the celestial bodies has to our knowledge of their respective distances, magnitudes, rotations, chemical constituents, etc., of all of which the animal is ignorant, although it sees the same bodies. May I be permitted to add that the materialist, whatever forces, energies, qualities, or attributes he may consider inherent in matter, tacitly admits the existence of mind as the superior source of knowledge, as often as he attempts to embrace any totality of phenomena in a logical formula.

It naturally follows, that only the sensual element of our knowledge consists of such images of facts or objects, which can be compared to their corresponding realties outside of the mind, and the truth of which, in the mind, is established beyond doubt, by geometry, arithmetic, physics, chemistry, &c., by the established facts of natural science. The mental element of our knowledge can not be compared with such realities, because it consists of no images thereof. With the man of history, the mental element preponderates over the sensual. Not by the intuition of his senses, he has his knowledge of God, the world as a cosmos in space and time with law, cause and effect, or of man as a race which makes history, or of the relations of God, man, and world. It is by the mental process that he knows whatever he may know, affirms or denies whatever he may do about God, man, world, and their relations. The sensual element is the minimum and the mental is the maximum in his knowledge. If the materialist denies the substantiality of the mind, he must nevertheless admit the reality of mental cognitions. For affirming or denying he exercises his mental judgment. In either case he must say, I think, and not I see, hear, smell, taste, or touch that your propositions about God, man, world, and their relations are true or false. If one speaks of the qualities of matter, he is already beyond the sphere of the sensual element and deals in abstractions. If one speaks of laws, mechanical, physical, or physiological, he stands upon a ground beyond the intuition of senses. If one thinks of religion, morals, government, law, art, science, taste, feeling, thought, will, talent, or genius, he deals in mental elements exclusively.

How do we know that what we mentally know is true? Is reasoning from analogy of the mental and sensual admissible? Are its conclusions reliable? A ball will roll down an inclined plane, and ideas will not. The association of ideas has nothing in common with the attraction of cohesion. Reason forms no judgment by mechanical action. All molecular motion of the brain is no thought yet. The laws of mind are entirely different from the laws of matter. One explains not the other. Therefore all supposed analogies to expound mind by matter or *vice versa*, the sensual by the mental element or *vice versa*, are necessarily false, the conclusions to which they lead must be illegitimate, and appear so also to the materialist who admits the existence of logic, the laws of which have nothing in common with the mechanical, physical, or physiological. Therefore, by reasoning from analogy we can not arrive at any certainty, that the mental elements of our knowledge are true.

Let us turn the question, how do we arrive at certainty that the sensual elements of our knowledge are true? All human senses are imperfect and liable to error. They are no accurate physical apparatuses, and we know that they are not. In numerous cases we do not trust our senses, and it is just that we do not, or we would still see in the sun a flat circular section thirty or forty feet in diameter a few thousand yards above our heads. We control the sensual impressions by mental reflection. We compare the preceptions with the mental ideas present in the mind, until the judgment produces harmony. We arrive at the certainty of shapes and distances by geometry, of numbers by arithmetic, of constituents by chemistry, of qualities and changes by physics, always by mental processes, controlling and correcting sensual impressions.

On the other hand, we reverse the process and say, the mental elements of our knowledge must be controlled and corrected by the sensual, until the mind arrives at the harmony of both. We know that our senses are imperfect physical apparatuses; hence we know more than the senses reveal, and we know better. This PLUS is the controlling power of all sensual intuitions. On the other hand, we see, hear, smell, taste, or touch sensual objects as shaped by imagination, and know that they are outside of us, as they appear to us. This knowledge of external realities must control and correct our speculations. Again we know that we know all this and that in one and the same self-consciousness, which acquires its knowledge of God, man, world, and their relations through two different avenues, to become one in the self-consciousness. Hence we can consider our knowledge correct and true, only if each idea is in harmony with all the others in the same self-consciousness. The sensual corrects the mental, the mental corrects the sensual, the process is reciprocal, until harmony is produced, which is truth.

The sensual elements of man's knowledge, composed of the images of material nature, formed by experience or experiments, controlled, harmonized, generalized, and systematized, and reduced to laws by the human intellect, is called natural science. You see, in science the sensual element is the substratum, upon which the mental works comparing and organizing. Science can not go beyond its sensual substratum, which it shapes. The mental elements of the mind, composed of the images of spirit, within and without, formed by observation, meditation and reflection, controlled and corrected by the sensual, harmonized, generalized, and systematized, is called philosopy. You see, in philosophy, the mental element is reason's substratum, upon which the sensual exercises a controlling and correcting influence. Philosophy is boundless as the human mind, and limited only by the facts of science and the laws of logic.

Here again the same criterion of truth. As long as science and philosophy contradict one another in any point or points, their dis-harmony proves inaccuracy or incompleteness of cognition on the one side or the other, and the necessity of correction. Their harmony is the only criterion of truth in our possession. Say in plain words, experience and speculation must control each other, and their harmony is to the human mind the criterion of truth in our knowledge. This rule will guide us invariably in this course of lectures. We will seek harmony in science and philosophy.

That the things outside of the mind really exist, can not be doubted in science; hence according to our criterion ot truth, it is established in philosophy. Immanuel Kant overthrows Berkeley's extreme idealism in the following thesis: "the mere consciousness, but empirically certain, of my own existence, proves the existence of objects in space outside of myself."* To prove means to show truth, in the light of certainty.

We add, to doubt the existence of things outside of mind is to doubt the truth and exactness of mathematics. If so, I must doubt every thing I know, for I know it all by one apparatus and by the same process. If my knowledge of the existence of things in space outside of me, is doubtful then my knowledge in general is doubtful, and this particular knowledge also must be doubtful; hence it is doubtful, that my knowledge of the existence of the things is doubtful. This is the vicious circle of skepticism, which at the last instance must doubt that it doubts.

In our opinion, man is gifted with all the powers to know truth and the full truth. That which we know now is no criterion of what man will know after ten thousand years of history. It can not be doubted that we know many things as certain as Descartes knew his "Cogito,ergo sum," and to know for certain is to possess truth in that matter. Whatever is possible is one department of our knowledge is possible in all of them. Let us seek truth and we will find it and recognize it by its criterion.

> " Truth, like a single point, escapes the sight,
> And claims attention to perceive it right;
> But what resembles truth is soon descried,
> Spreads like a surface, and expanded wide."

---

*Lehrsatz—Das blosse, aber empirish bestimmte, Bewusstein meines eigenen Daseines beweist das Dasein der Gegenstaende im Raum ausser mir.

LECTURE II.

THE MIND'S RECEPTIVITY AND SPONTANEITY.

LADIES AND GENTLEMEN.—If any one of you would feel the desire of presenting to your friend a bouquet, which by arrangement of colors and disposition of leaflets, should suggest in floral language your feelings and thoughts, you would certainly first go over your flower beds and select among Flora's offspring the most suitable to your purpose, then arrange and entwine them into a bouquet to your taste and wishes. Please imagine that I wish to present to you a bouquet of my best mental flowers, unfolding to you my thoughts and feelings. Must I not first go over my flower bed and make the proper selection? I only invite you to accompany me on a walk through the beautiful garden of human nature. Inductive philosophy is a systematic structure of harmonizing facts. First we must secure the facts, then we can construct the philosophical system. The substratum of all philosophy is the mental element of the mind; hence we must know all about it before we can philosophize. First the flowers and then the bouquet.

In my last lecture the work of collecting was commenced. I believe I have established that truth is ideal; it is in self-conscious intelligence only, relative and in proportion to the sum of each individual's knowledge; that this knowledge consists of sensual and mental elements and the harmony of these elements in the same consciousness is the criterion of truth. Let us see now how the mind obtains knowledge;—how do we come to know what we know.

The knowledge of every person is the aggregate of simple ideas, as none can think more than one idea at a time, which must be either received or spontaneous. Whatever one learns by oral instruction, letters, symbols, or examples consists of received ideas. Whatever one observes, experiences, within or without, discovers, invents, produces by meditation or reflection, is his own; and this knowledge consists of spontaneous ideas. Postulating mind as above, it follows that knowledge is obtained by two innate capacities of the mind, viz.: Receptivity and Spontaneity.

This proposition is not in conflict either with John Locke's or Immanuel Kant's respective theories. John Locke compares the soul to a blank sheet of paper, upon which will be that which will be written or printed on it. The comparison is false according to Locke's own opinions. If it were correct, then we must arrive at the knowledge of our knowledge and its elements by sensual observation only, so that if one had no corporeal senses he could possess no knowledge whatever, not even self-consciousness. This assertion is empiric, relies on external evidence, and yet there is none to support it. There never was known a human being without corporeal sense ; and if one had come under human observation, none could have ascertained his state of mind. On the other hand we know how the mind replaces to some extent a missing sense or senses, by the augmented abilities of the others, as among lower animals lost limbs are replaced, or teeth in young people, by the inherent organic force. The sense of touch or hearing with some blind people is perfectly wonderful and, to a great extent, replaces the lost sense of vision to the very distinction of colors. The facts collected in asylums for the deaf, dumb and blind, how senses or even limbs replace each other's activity and energy, by the internal organic force, are popularly known and need not be reproduced here.

The fact is that Locke himself protests only against innate maxims, in his time called innate ideas, adduced then to mystic speculations of all kinds; but he denies not the mind's innate capacities to know truth, or else nobody could possibly know, that there is any truth in sensual intuitions . What are those innate capacities of the mind, which Locke admits, enabling the mind to know truth ? They cannot be merely mechanical or chemical apparatuses to grasp, extort, press out or boil out truth or sensual impressions. They can be ideas only which are in the mind, conscious or unconscious, with which the new incomers are associated by their identity, or they are repelled as false by their dissimilarity. If so, the comparison to a sheet of paper is erroneous, for the capacities of the mind are active and essential, while the capacities of the paper are passive and accidental. Again, if so, there are ideas in the mind prior to sensual intuition, which must be spontaneous, besides those produced by meditation ; so that if there ever had been a man without any corporeal sense, he would still have thought over his own ideas or the imagery of his phantasy, as we see daily almost ignorant people do.

Therefore Kant, who had been considerably influenced by Locke's Essays, felt compelled to supplement Locke's theory by the fact that we arrive at the knowledge of our knowledge and its elements by inductive reasoning, starting from *a priori* ideas in the mind, to which the judgment compares every new idea acquired. The process appears somewhat mysterious, but it only appears so. I will try to show its simplicity and beauty.

But if there were, on this particular point any disagreement between Locke and Kant, Realism and Idealism, it would not impair my proposition. For if innate ideas be denied to the mind by any process of reasoning, its spontaneity must still be admitted, or else original ideas, inventions, and art would be impossible. An analysis of the process how man acquires knowledge affords us a clear insight into the mysterious laboratory. Here are facts perfectly mysterious and miraculous, and yet as plain as the seven colors of the rainbow.

Every word spoken, if attention is paid to it, forms an idea in the hearer's mind. Speaking produces waves in the air in the same manner as a stone cast into the water forms successive rings on its surface. These waves reach your ear, penetrate to its labyrinth, excite nerve and ganglion, set certain brain fibres in a tremulous motion, and become ideas in your mind. How are airy waves transformed into ideas? In speech as in music we hear no more than detached, simple sounds following one another in a more or less rapid succession; and yet the mind forms of these detached sounds, consecutive thoughts or melody, a complete story, argument, or harmonious and melodious music. Where or what is the mysterious force to produce the perfect unity of those detached sounds? Here are spontaneous processes of the mind, neither learned nor acquired, which produce ideas and a unity of ideas from mere detached sounds.

The same is the case with sight. The eye sees not the body which is the object of vision but the rays which the illuminated body reflects, and not all of them, indeed, but those which fall upon the cornea, and even some of these are reflected, while the others pass converged into the aqueous humor, then through the pupil, and impinge upon the lens, traverse the viterous humor, and are brought to a focus upon the nervous tunic, the hind wall of the eye, and there, as it were, is photographed a small and exact but inverted image of the object seen. We pass by the wonders of this most complicated organ and the mystery, how by a particular composition and arrangement of elementary matter, blind and thoughtless material is made to see and receive ideas, and consider for a moment the most mysterious facts of the process. How are ideas led to the mind by a few rays of light? You read a book *i. e.* you see certain rays of light reflected from the page, and your mind receives at the same time the thoughts, the wisdom, the highest and deepest researches of Moses or Aristotle, king Solomon or Darwin. Where is the connection between your mind and the black spots on the page called letters? Where is the connection between those black spots on the one hand and the author's mind on the other?

The same inexplicable mystery follows the act of vision throughout life. You see material objects, they pass away, but their images, the ideas, are retained in the mind. How can the objects seen form an idea in the mind? How are material objects transformed in a twinkle of the eye into ideas which are purely mental? How does the mind retain or reproduce them at various times, compare, classify, and unite them to general conceptions? From Aristotle to this day, the philosophers have attempted in vain the final solution of this mystery, and yet the same mystery precisely attaches to every corporeal sense and each sensation.

You see if Locke and the realists maintain that we arrive at the knowledge of our knowledge and its elements by sensation they have explained nothing, for they must stop short before the mystery of sensation and the unknown transformation of material objects into purely mental ideas.

Our theory, however, explains the matter as far as this is possible. We maintain, the mind is the apparatus which by its innate capacities, ideas themselves, receives and produces ideas. External objects, internal feelings, emotions and affects are mere impulses, or if you please symbols, to the mind, to set in motion corresponding ideas present in the mind. Without these impulses the mind would not form those ideas, *i. e.* it would not become conscious thereof; but then it would form others and similar ones; it would work upon the images of phantasy as children and ignorant persons often do, but think it must as the sun must shine. Therefore persons of two or even one corporeal sense do think, as experience teaches, and are capable of education.

As far, then, as we know by experience, the mind depends not in all cases on the senses, for the knowledge of its knowledge and the elements thereof. It possesses knowledge and exercises functions independent of the senses. The senses, however, depend on the functions of the mind. We know that the eye sees not the objects of sight. It could possibly see the image momentarily impressed on the nervous wand; but this is exceedingly dimunitive, flat and inverted, the very thing which we see not; hence the eye sees not; it is a mere instrument for another apparatus of vision, as the spectacles, the microscope and telescope are artificial eyes for the eye. The optic nerve, the ganglia and the brain fibres, in the cavity of the head beyond the reach of light, certainly can not see, as there can be no vision without light. Hence the legitimacy of the question, what sees? I have knocked at the door of all physicists and physiologists and none gave me a satisfactory answer, what sees? Therefore I could only fall back upon our theory, the mind sees. Every body almost knows that many a day a number of objects and persons pass his sight without his notice, and the same is the case with hearing and all other sensations; because he paid no attention to them, because his mind did not see or hear, it was otherwise engaged, and none can think two ideas at the same time.

How does the mind see or hear and retain the objects perceived? or in other words, how is matter transformed into purely mental ideas? Matter becomes perceptible to the senses by its qualities, *i. e.*, by the ideas which it represents. Each quality is an idea. Thus every object represents a number of ideas which it embodies. The mind perceives not matter itself, but the simple ideas which it represents, and combines them, to a unit identical with the object of sensation, as shaped by the imagination. The intelligence then forms the word and the imagination the corresponding picture. Therefore we cannot perceive chaos, it represents no ideas; and where but one idea presents itself, as in the air, we see nothing except this one idea.

How does the mind know that the word and picture thus formed are correct, identical with the object. Here come in Kant's *a priori Begriffe*, or Locke's innate capacities of the mind to know truth, together with my criterion of truth. Matter is not transformed into mind, for we perceive only the ideas which it embodies. The same is the case not only with all sensual intuitions, but also with all internal sensations, feelings, emotions, and affects of which we become conscious only if the mind forms the ideas to which they give the impulse; if we know not pain, we have none; if we know not joy, we feel none.

You see, ladies and gentlemen, the great problem, how do we obtain our knowledge, how do we come to know what we know, can be solved only by the word MIND. The mind with its capacities of receptivity and spontaneity accounts for our knowledge. It might be urged, that all animals must possess mind, which we have no reason here to deny or discuss. I will investigate this subject in another lecture. Here I must yet say in conclusion, that materialists have attempted another solution of this problem; but I discuss this in the next lecture. To foreshadow coming arguments, I call your attention to the following passage in Prof. Tydall's Inaugural Address called "Advancement of Science" (New York edition, page 49:

"Thus far our way is clear, but now comes my difficulty. Your atoms are individually without sensation, much more are they without intelligence. May I ask you, then, to try your hand upon this problem. Take your dead hydrogen atoms, your dead oxygen atoms, your dead carbon atoms, your dead nitrogen atoms, your dead phosphorus atoms, and all the other atoms, dead as grains of shot, of which the brain is formed. Imagine them seperate and sensationless; observe them running together and forming all imaginable combinations; this as a purely mechanical process, is *seeable* by the mind. But can you see, or dream, or in any way imagine, how out of that mechanical act, and from these individually dead atoms, sensation, thought, and emotion are to arise? You speak, of the difficulty of mental presentation in my case; is it less in yours? I am not all bereft of this *Vorstellungs-kraft* of which you speak. I can follow a particle of musk until it reaches the olfactory nerve; I can follow the waves of sound until their tremors reach the water of the labyrinth, and set the otoliths and Corti's fibers in motion; I can also visualize the waves either as they cross the eye or hit the retina. Nay, more, I am able to follow up to the central organ the motion thus imparted at the periphery, and to see in idea the very molecules of the brain thrown into tremors. My insight is not baffled by these physical processes. What baffles me, what I find unimaginable, transcending every faculty I possess—transcending, I humbly submit, every faculty *you* possess—is the notion that out of those physical tremors you can extract things so utterly incongruous with them, as sensation, thought, and emotion. You may say, or think, that this issue of consciousness from the clash of atoms is not more incongruous than the flash of light from the union of oxygen and hydrogen. But I beg to say it is. For such incongruity as the flash possesses is that which I now force upon your attention. The flash is an affair of consciousness, the objective counterpart of which is a vibration. It is a flash only by our interpretation. *You* are the cause of the apparent incongruity; and *you* are the thing that puzzles me. I need not remind you that the great Leibnitz felt the difficulty which I feel, and that to get rid of this monstrous deduction of life from death he displaced your atoms by his monads, and which were more or less perfect mirrors of the universe, and out of the summation and integration of which he supposed all phenomena of life—sentient, intellectual, and emotional—to arise. Your difficulty, then, as I see you are ready to admit, is quite as great as mine. You can not satisfy the human understanding in its demand for logical continuity between molecular processes and the phenomena of consciousness. This is a rock on which materialism must inevitably split whenever it pretends to be a complete philosophy of life."

LECTURE III.

MIND OR BRAIN.

LADIES AND GENTLEMEN.—If a stranger coming to this city should not know its name, and on inquiry be told by every body asked, it is Cincinnati, he would certainly be obliged to believe it on account of the common consent pointing to a fact otherwise probable. In case, however, that stranger should dispute the fact, it would be his task to prove that all his informants were in error. We Cincinnatians would only say, ask any body else and he will tell you that this is Cincinnati. The same precisely is the case with the materialistic hypothesis, "The brain thinks." The vastest majorities of all civilized and half civilized nations, ancient and modern, and among them the most prominent men of all ages of authentic history have believed and established philosophically, "The mind thinks," hence the materialist denying this must furnish the evidence in support of his theory.

Besides we know already that every natural object presents itself to human cognition by the ideas, inherent in the object represented. So there is ideality, or spirituality, if you please, in every natural object, or else man could not possibly conceive it.

Again, if man is the object of our observation, we must hold up steadily before our mind, two distinct kinds of qualities.

He presents to us bodily qualities and peculiarities, by which we know him as a material object—and a character; he is kind, generous, magnanimous, unselfish, heroic, pious, moral, sympathetic, intelligent, genial, loving, amiable, wise or otherwise, and in all that we contemplate qualities which have not the least similarity to the qualities of matter. We contemplate his mental and moral character, and each of us is conscious that he is in possession of similar qualities. Therefore if the materialist denies mind, it is for him to prove that the qualities which make the particular character of man are inherent in matter, and having succeeded in this, he must prove, that the qualities of matter are material, and not idealistic or spiritualistic, as we maintain; and having succeeded in all this, he must furnish us at least with a probable theory of sensation, perception, conception, and cognition; which all materialists admit, they can not do.

It is not my intention to discuss here this problem in all its bearings; I restrict my remarks to the simple proposition: Materialism with its physical, mechanical, and chemical laws does not and can not account for the knowledge of our knowledge and its elements; and wherever the attempt is made, it takes invariably the effect for the cause. Physiological functions, which are evidently effects of some cause, are invariably and unphilosophically held up as causes of that, of which they appear as effects, and must appear so to the strictest scientist.

Please cast a glance upon this keynote of all materialistic physiology:—"The brain is the seat and organ of thought,"—Mr. Buechner exclaims: "Its quantity, form, and chemical peculiarities are in direct proportion to the greatness and force of its mental functions."

If all this were true, as it is not, it would prove just as well, that the brain is the organ of the thinking mind, which, in proportion to its greatness and force, provides itself with an adequate organ, as the organic force provides a stomach for the animal adequate to its bulk. Or it would prove that in proportion with the mind's activity of any individual, the blood supplies the brain, which accordingly increases in bulk, improves in shape, and absorbs from the blood the best molecules for its purpose, as do the blacksmith's arms or the mountaineer's legs. In both cases, however, mind is the cause and brain the effect. No physiologist has examined the brain before it thought and then observed its stages of improvement with the progression of mind, to establish scientifically upon facts observed, how thoughts and judgments grow out of certain brain cells, filled up or divided in the process of growth. But if that could be done, we would still be ignorant on the point of cause, for we would have effects only. The brain is not its own cause, that is certain; and if it were only the cause of thought, it must be able to contemplate itself, as is evidently the nature of mind; yet nobody knows his own brain or could ever contemplate it except by comparison with other brains. We maintain, the action of the brain has a cause and is an effect; and the materialist maintains, it is a causeless cause, certainly in all spontaneous thoughts and original ideas. It is an anomaly.

How does the materialist arrive at his brain hypothesis? By comparison of the human brain with that of animals, and various human brains among themselves. Let us see what the facts are. The quantity of brain is no proof of superior intellect, for the whale's brain, according to Rudolphi, weighs five and one-third pounds, two pounds more than the largest human brain; and the elephant, according to Perault, carries nine pounds of brain in his skull. Still nobody maintains that those animals are man's equal in intelligence. R. Wagner has given the subject a thorough investigation, and has tabularized the brains of a thousand persons according to weight. It was discovered that Cromwell, Byron, and Cuvier had the heaviest brains, although none will seriously maintain that they were the most intellectual men; and far below them in weight are classed some of the most eminent reasoners. If the big head would make the wise man, then the hatter must be the best judge of human intelligence. The proportion of brain weight to human intelligence must evidently be dropped.

Next comes the proportion of brain to the bulk of the body, which they say decides the intelligence. Man has, in proportion to his body, the heaviest brain. So the materialists, with due politeness, save female intelligence, as woman's brain is lighter than man's, but it is in proportion to her body. If that proportion were true, then man stands below many little birds in the scale of intelligence; and according to Cuvier, also below several families of monkeys, whose brain stands in proportion to their bodies as one to twenty-eight, one to twenty-four, or even one to twenty-two; while with man the relation is as one to thirty, or even thirty-five. Unfortunate in this direction is the observation of Volkman, that the smallest and young animals have relatively the largest brains, so that in animals there is no proportion between intellect and the size of the brain; consequently every conclusion of this kind from animal to man is certainly illegitimate. Worse than this are the simple facts well known of bees, wasps, ants, and spiders, which have no brain at all, and yet their intelligence is admired. If the nerve-knots of those little creatures secrete intelligence, then it is independent of brain anyhow.

It must be remarked here that the proportion of the spinal column to the diameter of the brain also is not in favor of man, for in man this proportion is as seven to one, and in the dolphin, according to Cuvier, as thirteen to two, or as six and eleven-twelfths to one according to Thiedman.

Next comes the argument derived from the proportion of the cerebellum to the cerebrum and its convolutions. Weight, we have seen, decides nothing. Still it is maintained that man's cerebrum, having the most and deepest convolutions, and being so much larger in proportion to the cerebellum, than in any animal, therefore man possesses so much more intellectual power. Longet, however, states plainly that, according to Cuvier's and Leuret's results in this research, the proportion of cerebrum to cerebellum is no reliable phenomenon, as this would place man intellectually on a level with the ox, and even below the *Sapaju*.

In regard to the convolutions it must be remarked that an ancient physician, Erasistratus, maintained that convolutions are more numerous in man's brains than in any other, because man possesses intelligence and the animal does not. Galenus, however, refutes this hypothesis; he shows that the brain of the ass has numerous convolutions without bearing any particular reputation for prominent intelligence. Leuret and Gratiolet, who gave this matter particular attention, show that many mammals, standing intellectually as high as others, have no convolutions in the brain; and Leuret especially denies the whole theory based upon the convolutions. But suppose the fact established that the most intellectual beings show the most and deepest convolutions of the brain, what does it amount to? Certainly no more than this, that the activity of the intellect leaves its impress on the brain. Convolutions can not think, since they are nothing but empty furrows which work no change in the internal construction of the brain.

What is the actual value of the whole argument taken from the morphology of the brain? It is intended to prove that man's superior intellect is observeable in the superior construction of his brain, consequently the brain is the cause of the intelligence. But the first member of the proposition is by no means certain, as we have seen man's brain can not boast of any distinction so marked as to account for his superior intelligence. If it did actually bear all the morphological distinction claimed it would still not be established that the brain is the cause of intelligence. It would not lead one step beyond our starting-point, unless it be proved that brain matter secretes thought, that the purely material substance brings forth the purely mental thought, or in other words that matter is changed into mind. And also then the question would arise, whether the mind flashing forth from the action of organic matter is not an individual dynamic force, self-existing and imperishable.

Driven from morphology, the materialist resorts to chemistry and pathology to make good his assertion. It is the peculiar chemical composition which constitutes the superiority of the human brain. Commonly brain contains seventy-five and one-half per cent. of water, seven per cent. albuminous matter, eleven and one-half per cent. of fat, one and one-half per cent. of phosphoric, and four and one-half per cent. of other salts. The proportion of these constituents varies in different brains. The brains of insane persons were found decreased in weight as low as two pounds, and the salts, especially phosphoric acid, were much exhausted. Therefore Moleshot exclaimed, "No thought without phosphorus." Liebig contradicted it; and Bibra, who made this point a special study, refuted the whole chemical theory, as practical physicians of insane asylums did with the pathological point. Phosphoric acid is a compound of phosphorus and oxygen, hence no thought without oxygen. This is indeed too trivial and frivolous a point to be discussed. For after we know full well the chemical constituents of every brain, we have not yet the remotest idea how elementary matter so arranged and mixed can think. We still deal in effects, and bandage our eyes to the cause. After we know all pathological effects on the brain, we are no wiser than before, because we know not the cause which produces the degeneracy of the brain.

You see, ladies and gentlemen, there is not one established point in morphology, chemistry, or pathology which justifies the assertion that the brain thinks without a dynamic force at its foundation for which it is the organ. Let us now see whether any thinking person can form a clear and intelligent idea how the brain thinks. The sensations, by the aid of the senses, nerves, and ganglia, impress, or rather imprint upon the brain images which represent ideas, so that there are as many imprints on the tissues of the brain as we have ideas, received through the senses from without or the feelings from within. This is the materialistic theory of sensation, which, in my opinion, is as unphilosophical as it is unscientific. It rests neither upon facts observed nor upon any sort of legitimate speculation. For in the first place the mind is not passive to receive impressions as wax or plaster of Paris. If the mind makes no assertion, pays no attention, it receives no impressions by the senses. And in the second place, not one impression of the brain has been microscopically examined and identified with any idea whatever; still this alone would justify the theory and give it a scientific aspect. The facts of phrenology, as far as they are established, prove nothing in this direction, and are entitled to no other legitimate conclusion than this: Either particular faculties of the mind require certain inborn brain organs through which to operate, or those faculties by exercise and exertion develope certain brain parts more fully and prominently. .

The theory fares worse, the closer we inspect and analyze it. Unphilosophical minds imagine the whole process a sort of telegraph without telegraphist. The senses telegraph their impressions to the brain via the sensory nerves, and the brain telegraphs back its decision and will via the motory nerves. They do not trouble themselves with the questions, how colors, odors, feelings, or even sounds can be telegraphed, or where the battery has been discovered, how it is fed, and excited to action by sensations, feelings or volitions. But they go on and say, that every sensation makes its imprint on the brain, to remain there until crowded out by others, when the former are forgotten. It never occurs to their minds, that the supposed telegraphing process actually explains nothing and is a mere play on words; for after all the making and retaining of the impressions in the brain and their appearance in the consciousness are no less wonderful and unaccounted for than without the telegraphing hypothesis. .

Let us examine a little closer. The particles of the body, hence also of the brain, are subject to perpetual change. According to modern experiments, the whole body, every particle thereof, is completely changed in every two years. Therefore one should think, that the brain atoms with all impressions on them are subject to the same change. Now, if one or more atoms in a man's brain bear the image of his wife, the atom or atoms being gone two years after his marriage, the brain record being wiped out, that man must not only forget that he ever was married, but he must be incapable of recognizing his wife. Yet memory leads us back to the very morn of childhood, the dawn of consciousness, and no honest man forgets his wife, or his obligations.

Says the materialist, the particles change but not the individual; the form, the *morphe*, remains unchanged so also the brain impressions, although small scars on the skin will certainly disappear altogether. Let us see, how that is possible. The impression must be somewhere in in the brain, and the particle or atom bearing it must leave some time, to be replaced by another deposited there by the blood. We can only imagine the parting atom has the politeness or kindness, to inform its successor of the particular record which it bears. But then every atom must be intelligent, and man has as many souls as his brain has atoms. The elementary matter of the brain differing in no wise from other matter, it follows that all atoms are intelligent; *ergo* the universe consists of intelligent atoms, or to speak intelligibly, say, what we idealists call matter, is imaginary only, it is all intelligence, all mind; the universe is an *e pluribus unum*, a conglomeration of atomistic minds, each very small, of course, but with some extension after all. The only difficulties are, to account for irrationality of inorganic matter, and the harmony in the cosmos of those infinite numbers of intelligence atoms. Is this absurd enough to refute itself?

Look upon the matter from another point, if you please. Man has judgment. No materialist denies this. Judgment, so to say, presides over the ideas, compares, combines, or separates them, hears their testimony, and distinguishes between truth and error, right and wrong, good and evil, etc. This is evidently no offspring of sensual intuition. Where in the brain is that judgment? Says the materialist, it is in the brain center, in the sensorium, as though science could furnish any knowledge about it, anatomical, physiological, chemical, mechanical or physical. Still let us suppose for a moment, there is such a thing actually as a brain center or sensorium gifted with the function of judgment. It can be no vacuum hence it must consist of one or more atoms gifted with the capacity of judgment. Science has no knowledge of such atoms. Plato had his ideas, Liebnitz his monades, the dualist his soul, and the materialist his particular atoms gifted with judgment; where is really the difference?

But there comes in again the fact of perpetual change of matter, the tissue metamorphosis, inseparable from organic life. Now the question is simply this, are those judgment atoms also liable to this process or are they not. If they are not, then we have in man an imperishable, intelligent judgment—gifted something, not liable to change, which the materialist calls a particular atom and we call it mind, spirit, soul; the thing is the same, and our dispute is amicably settled. But if judgment atom or atoms are subject to the same law as others, they must be replaced from time to time by the blood, *i. e.* the blood must prepare those particular atoms and deposit them at the right time in the proper place. Then the judgment is in the blood, which the brain can neither control nor direct, its circulation being independent of the brain action. But the blood depends on stomach and lung, hence the seat of judgment is in the stomach and in the lung. But these two organs depend on food and atmosphere for all atoms received and sent to the blood; *ergo* the seat of judgment is in the food and the atmospheric air. I hope Prof. John Tyndal will comprehend the absurdities, in which atomism must finally land.

Last though not least, the original question turns up again; viz: if we admit all alleged facts and conclusions of materialism, how do we know that what we know is true? All human senses, as physical apparatuses, are notoriously defective; we know that they are, and justly mistrust them. They do not perceive all phenomena in nature, nor do they always perceive correctly. Therefore we must assist our senses with various instruments, and also control one by another. Then the sensory nerves lead the sensations to the brain. Are they reliable? We know no difference of texture of the optic, auditory and olfactory nerves, although their functions are so entirely different; how can we know the reliability of the nervous function? We know they are subject to changes and impairing influences, and like the senses they can be vastly improved by practice. Where is the certainty, that the nerves lead correctly the images of sensation to the brain? There is none. Then the brain itself is not excepted from all those deficiencies. Imagination overpowers it, and it sees, hears, feels, or smells nonentities. Sleep overcomes it and it dreams fictions. In a state of hallucination it takes phantasmagories for realities. A glass of wine changes its function. Where is the guarantee, that senses, nerves, ganglia, and brain perceive correctly? There is none. Imperfect organs can not form perfect ideas. The common consent of many or all, in this relation, proves nothing, as all are the same men with the same deficient organs of sensation. If one superior to man would assure us that we see the things correctly; we might be induced to believe him; but if we tell one another, it amounts to nothing in reality.

Here evidently intelligence, mind is necessary, to control senses, nerves, ganglia, and brain, to judge and correct the sensual intuitions. This is the ultimatum; either it must be admitted, the mind controls and corrects the sensual intuitions, or it must be confessed, that all science, mathematics included, is uncertain, and unreliable. No sound reasoner will admit this latter alternative; therefore the knowledge of our knowledge and its elements necessitates us to acknowledge the existence of mind.

We have now the whole force of circumstantial evidence on the side of the mind as the bearer of intelligence, and could dismiss this subject. We have found a starting point to our system: There is mind. But I mean to go beyond this, and seek conclusive and final evidence for our postulate, and then build upon it deductively a system of philosophy as far and as well as I am capable of solving the problems.

LECTURE IV.

HUMAN MIND ACTUALIZED IN ITS MONUMENTS.

LADIES AND GENTLEMEN,— The scientist tells us, this material universe consists of matter and force, without confessing that we know not, to any degree of certainty, outside of the mind's final decisions, whether their qualities are in matter or in the mind which thinks them. Again the absolute nature of force is beyond the present powers of experimental science. We call force any cause which produces or tends to produce a change in a body's state of rest or motion, and define its statical or dynamical measure, without any knowledge of the substance or *quodity* of force. Still we speak with perfect certainty of the existence of gravitation, cohesion, elasticity, chemical affinity, and the other forces, because we observe their influences on matter and the changes produced; and the mind is certain of the law of causality.

I will not trouble you now with an examination of the law of causality, although I will have to do it some other time; I will merely call your attention, in the first place, to two points:

1. We have no knowledge of the substance of any natural force, and no empiric knowledge of the existence of any.
2. Postulating the law of causality we arrive inductively at the conclusion that any force exists, because it is actualized in a phenomenon.

Take away point second, and science is impossible; especially as the main object of all science is to discover the laws of nature by the guiding compass of the law of causality.

Please, ladies and gentlemen, let us change terms for a little while. Let us put mind in place of force, and call it mind-force. Then let us put in place of the physical such mental phenomena in which mind-force is actualized. Let us contemplate those monuments in which the human mind has become permanently objective, and I expect we shall arrive at the conclusion:—

By the application of the strictest scientific method, basing upon the law of causality, to the monuments of the human mind, its existence is proved beyond a doubt.

Which are the main monuments or mental phenomena in which the human mind has become permanently objective? I answer: language, history, art, science, religion, and philosophy.

In the various (about twelve hundred) languages the spirit of man has become objective, crystalized, photographed, concrete, and tangible. Whatever a nation thought, felt or did, the character, intelligence, occupation, aspiration, ethical and aesthetical feelings, the whole of man of every age and clime is portrayed in the nation's dialect or dialects. Every language contains the history of its originators.

It has been asserted that animals, and birds, especially, have the use of language, to which, I must add, they possess the capacity of uttering certain sounds which were erroneously called language. These are simply vowel sounds, which do not go beyond the interjection. This is not language. Man utters four kinds of sounds, commonly called screaming, whistling, singing and speaking, of which the latter only consists of articulate sounds. Most of the animals scream, some, and especially birds, whistle; very few of them possess the capacity of singing rythmical melody. In all cases the utterances consist of simple vowel sounds, without discernable consonants. Man only possesses all the capacities of uttering sounds, and produces language by the combination of vowels with consonants; which no animal does.

Syllables are vowels encased in consonants, and every language consists of its syllables; therefore man alone possesses language. There are physiological causes for this phenomenon, which I can not explain now.

The main characteristic of language is, the almost infinite combinations of about twenty-five consonantal sounds with the vowels. Language, you see, is combination, the offspring of judgment, to express intelligibly man's ideas. The substance of language is not in the elementary sounds; A B C is no language; it is in the free combination thereof to express ideas. There is nothing material in it; it is all actualized mind. In form language is grammatical, and must be so to be language. It must have substantive, verb, and adjective, subject, object, and copula, cases, persons, and tenses. The grammatical form is as inseparable from the substance of language as form is from organic matter in any organism. Therefore it is certainly an error to speak of the language of animals. Still, in this connection, it could make no difference to us if animals had language. It would merely prove that animals must possess mind; and the superiority of human language would be the evidence of the superiority of the human mind. Anyhow language would be the monument of actualized mind. We claim no more.

There are two mysteries connected with language which however, explain one another. I refer to the origin and and common intelligibility of language. How did men understand each other's sounds? How do we understand one another? How are sounds or signs converted into ideas? I know of but one reply to this query: The mind possesses the innate ability to form words for objects, feelings, etc., and the necessity of representing them by sounds or signs. Therefore the word spoken or read excites the mind to form a corresponding idea, and the idea is instantly actualized in the word which caused it, so that every word heard or read with attention is the cause of the rise of the corresponding idea in the listening or reading subject. Therefore we do not retain words of which the mind has formed no definite idea, so that the word is actually dead. It is precisely the same as with sensation in general. The outward object can not enter the mind. It gives the impulse to the formation of a corresponding idea in the mind, of which the imagination shapes the image, and the intelligence furnishes the word.

It follows, therefore, that the mind makes words also, without having seen or heard them, as children and deaf mutes frequently make words of their own. The objects of sensation necessitate the mind to form ideas which must be marked by words. If we ask, how did language originate? The reply is simple and given correctly in the Bible. When Adam saw the various animals, his mind was necessitated to form ideas of them, which became images in his imagination and words in his intelligence. So language originated, man named objects, actions, relations, feelings, and thoughts; and it is of divine origin only as far as man's mind is. The languages and dialects have their origin in the geographical separation of the various tribes. Also in this point the Bible advances the correct idea.

Language is not the product of mechanical brain action. This is evident from the freedom in the choice of sounds and combinations to denote the same object in various tongues and dialects. There is no freedom imaginable in connection with mechanical causes. If we even admit that the utterance of elementary sounds, as with animals, is the effect of mechanical brain action; the combination of sounds to denote objects, etc., requires judgment, free choice, definite and conscious purpose, for which no kind of mechanism is imaginable. Ed. von Hartman commits the error of confounding the origin of a language with the origin of the words constituting it. Words are produced consciously; the language is built up unconsciously by countless individuals who contributed to its wealth. It is no less an error, although Professor Steinthal also adopted it, that the feelings were the primary causes of language. The mechanical screams caused by feelings are simple interjections, whose signification is in the peculiarity of the sound, and not in the definite idea conveyed by any word; and language consists of such words. The O! or Ah! may convey the idea of joy, pain, admiration, surprise, astonishment, longing, or almost any other feeling, depending altogether on the momentary sound. Men could never begin to understand one another by the tradition of the mere modulations of indefinite sounds. Only after a feeling or sensual impression had become an idea in the mind, the adequate word could have been formed, to rouse in other minds the corresponding idea, say of any tree, animal, or love, hatred, etc; not because tree or animal excited a feeling, but because it conveyed a number of ideas to the mind of which it produced a unity in one word. The same process is observable in children. The origin of language can neither be thought nor imagined without the pre-existence of judgment, hence of mind.

Here then is a phenomenon, a grand effect purely mental. Here are your twelve hundred different languages and dialects. Here are your libraries, the millions of books and manuscripts, containing the highest wisdom of man. Here are your inscriptions on stones, tombs, pyramids, bricks and coins, reaching clear back to the cradle of humanity. Here are facts without precedent or parallel in organic or inorganic nature, grand, original, and eminently human, monuments in which human mind has become objective in such incalculable quantity, that we can think of no number to designate the ideas crystalized therein. In these monuments the objectivity of the human mind stands before our intelligence as clear, undeniable, doubtless, concrete, and tangible as static or dynamic force in any physical phenomenon of daily occurrence; and no naturalist can justly tell us that our induction from mind-phenomena is less legitimate or less certain than his induction of force from physical phenomena.

The next monument of the actualized mind is HISTORY. History is the term under which we understand a narrative of the experience of the human family; what man did and suffered, established and destroyed, gained and lost, together with all means employed against uproarious and destructive elements, his combat against hostile and ferocious beasts, his wars, defeats, victories, the entire life, developement, progressions, retrogressions, and triumphs of the human race, in which the fates and experiences of individuals, tribes, and nations, and the records of governments, churches, institutions, sciences, arts, and philosophy are like the members of one grand organism, each of which is inseparable from the whole, which is an organic unit. The substance of history is the human mind actualized, and all institutions are its framework. Mind-force has produced myriads of mental phenomena, which, in their totality, are the history of the human race.

If we go back three centuries only in this country, we have before our mind an unbroken wilderness of forests and prairies from ocean to ocean, with a few thousand sons of the desert, who fought the same battles against the elements and beasts, as thousands of years ago the whole human family did. All were like the savage Indians and in much lower conditions, still more helpless as we come down to the stone age, although not all at the same time precisely. If now we compare our flourishing country with its free government, its laws, institutions, farms, gardens, villages, cities, works of art and genius, highways, canals, railroads, industry, commerce, prosperity, security, peace, and confidence, to the state of affairs three hundred years ago, we have an index to the history of mankind, which took probably five thousand to six thousand years to pass through all those phases of developement, to reach the culture and civilization of the nineteenth century.

In history, we behold the human mind crystalized in deeds. Just think of the vast amount of thought expended, of inventions made, of schemes and projects proposed, of calculations and combinations spun out, before the soil was conquered for the plough, the forces and materials of nature subjected to human hands, and man was sufficiently cultivated to govern himself and the objects of physical nature. It is uncountable, incalculable, almost infinite; and yet every idea is permanent, and the best ones are imperishable in history, as the atoms of this physical world. As this earth consists of its atoms by the inherent force of cohesion, so history consists of innumerable ideas coherent by their internal force of psychical affinity, which we will call the Genius of History. As the coal fields now utalized, contain in the materialized form, the heat issuing, many thousands of years ago, from the sun, and combining with the carbon; so the original ideas of all individuals and ages were actualized, so to say materialized, to be preserved intact as the ever progressive history of man.

Every body almost knows, that there is at the bottom of man's doings and omissions the law of self-preservation and the preservation of the race, together with the social instinct, which man has in common with animals. But this explains not the Genius of History; for these animal qualities did not make history, did not produce the thoughts and inventions which are the substance of history; nor did they combine and connect them to the organic unit of cause and effect, as history presents, upon the pinnacle of which, as its last and legitimate result, appears the *facit* in the civilization and culture of this nineteenth century. Animals with those instincts, and in many instances demonstrably stronger than man's, offer no history and no material of history, with the slightest analogy to what we have just defined as man's history. One must forcibly and willfully bandage his mental eyes, if he maintains not to see, that physiological causes, Darwinism or no Darwinism, can not and do not account for the history of man. Physical and mechanical causes are certainly out of question, where uncountable millions of free agents, each working out his own destiny, first and foremost taking care of himself, separated in time and space, and mostly knowing nothing or little of one another, still work out one common destiny, one logos of history, one and the same end, aim and purpose of perpetual progression, and continual perfectation, a unit of purpose as is the earth a unit of atoms. Here physical and mechanical laws find no application.

Therefore, I ask, what is at the bottom of the pyramid

of history? which is the force uniting the isolated ideas of all the millions to the one, incomparable and admirable structure? Mind, mind, mind! there is no other answer, no other key to solve this mystery. It is mind-force which produces these phenomena and their most wonderful union. Here are the phenomena and induction from them to their cause is certainly as legitimate here as in natural science. If scientists would study philology, in the modern sense of the term, and history more carefully, there could be no materialism.

We must postpone the discussion of the other topics to our next lecture. Before we close, I must say, that here lies one fault, and it is a serious one of our American colleges and universities; they neglect philology and history. The principle of immediate utility, concrete selfishness, advances materialism and superstition as the necessary extremes. Enlightened minds think clearly and independently; utilized brains are self-supporting machines. Students must be first enlightened minds, pillars of truth.

LECTURE V.

HUMAN MIND ACTUALIZED IN ITS MONUMENTS.

PART II.

LADIES AND GENTLEMEN,—Let us spend a short time, in the conclusion of our subject, investigating the monuments in which human mind has become actualized, let us take into consideration art and science, religion and philosophy. None can think of the fine arts without connecting them with talent, to construct a harmonious unit from elaborate details; or genius, to conceive harmonious unity spontaneously, neither of which can be conceived without the principle of mind, and a high degree of ideality therein. More even than the fine arts, the mechanical and useful arts, in connection with science, demonstrate the existence of mind, a power in man superior to all natural forces known to science.

Linne advanced the hypothesis, the vegetable kingdom is the final cause of the earth. The graminivorous animals were made to crop off the superfluous grass, the carnivorous to limit the increase of the former, and man to keep the latter within proper bounds. The only question not answered is, Why did the earth not limit the increase of plants by her own energies, and save the trouble of bringing forth man and beast? I have to add, if such was the intention of dame nature, then she made a grievous mistake, for man governs and exterminates not only most of the animals not specially useful to him, but also numerous families of the vegetable kingdom by the progress of agriculture, which gradually subjects the earth's habitable surface to the hands of man.

If anything on this earth besides man was creation's final cause, then man frustrates that intention. The agriculturist or mariner, craftsman or mechanic, continually counteracts the earth's primary designs, and governs natural forces, as the lightning-rod bids defiance to the shock of the electric current, steam to the force of gravitation, electricity to distance, optical instruments to the weakness of the eye, under the hands of man and his creative genius. True, the mind creates no material, but it brings forth ideas; it invents combinations, appropriates and applies matter and is forces; it is creative power after all.

By the practical arts, which reach far beyond the records of history, down into the stone age, man becomes free and makes himself the lord of the earth. As he progresses in science and art, he extends his dominion, increases his prosperity and comfort, enlarges his sphere of knowledge and enlightment, and subjects all things to his purposes. If there is anything in the book of Genesis which deserves more admiration even than Mr. Haeckel lavishes on the Mosaic account of creation, it is the blessing which, it is said there, the Creator bestowed on man: "And subdue it (the earth), and have dominion over the fishes of the sea and the birds of the air," etc., which inspired the poet to sing the beautiful Psalm viii. Now, in this age of hydro-oxygen gas and electric light, of spectrum analysis, solar photography, microscopic and telescopic researches, now those words are intelligle to us. Yes, in this age of the Suez Canal, St. Go'hard and Pacific railroads, transmarine cables, swimming palaces on rivers and oceans, and flying mansions on *terra-firma*, we see clearly how the spirit of man has wrestled all night with the spectre of dark and dire necessity, and man has prevailed; although lame yet, still the sun has risen, and he has prevailed. It hardly need be said any more than man's prosperity and progress depend on his success in the subjugation of matter and its forces to the creations of the mind, or that these successes are achieved with every passing day, as every intelligent child might know and even see it.

Again, as it is the object of the practical arts to subdue and govern matter and its forces, it is the object of science to discover the laws of nature which govern elements and forces, and by incorporating them in man's consciousness, enlarge his sphere of knowledge, and enlighten his understanding. Every new discovery is an idea added to the wealth of the mind, which discovers the law in the correlation of ideas and the constancy of phenomena. The more discoveries the better we are enabled to construct laws, and so much more thorough and complete is our knowledge of nature's secret labratory; and so much more is it ours, at our disposal, subject to human mind. It is self-evident that man comprehends nature's elements, forces, and laws, and they comprehend him not; hence, he actually possesses them, and they possess him not.

Here we have an undeniable something, in both art and science, which is superior to nature's elements, forces, and laws. It understands them, and they understand him not. It possesses them, and they possess him not. It governs, applies, and modifies them to his ends and purposes. What is it, this nameless something? Science with all its excellency, achievements, and redeeming qualities, does not and can not tell us what it is, and yet it must admit that it is entirely different in its manisfestations from all objects which yield to experimental science. It observes, discerns, discovers, analyzes, combines, and constructs laws; it is intelligent. It applies and invents; it (is creative. It subjects, reigns, rules, governs; it is will and power. Hence here is a nameless something, which is creative intelligence and motive will. What objection can any exact scientist have if we call it mind? I know of no more appropriate name. Therefore, I maintain, art and science are the monuments of human mind, in which it is perpetually actualized.

Mind reaches its loftiest and most lustrous objectivity, when turned from the material universe, it plunges into its own mysterious depth and contemplates itself; then, by its unmeasurable buoyancy, it breaks through the narrow compass of self, soars aloft from truth to truth to the highest truth, through the dark regions of the phenomenal world, of cause and effect, to the region of eternal light, life, love and wisdom, where all which is, was, or will be, meets at the crystal fountain-head, dissonances vanish, and all elements and forms of existence melt into one grand harmony. There and then mind contemplates itself in the mirror of universal mind, and reaches the sublimity of self-consciousness, self-knowledge, *a priori.* This self-contemplation and self-elevation, guided by spontaneous inspiration, is religion; guided by discoursive reason, it is philosophy. The verities which religion spontaneously produced, form the substance to which philosophy gives form and unity. Formal philosophy produces nothing; it groups organically, proves and disproves, systematizes, shapes, forms, produces unity out of chaos, silences dissonances, and swells the accords of ideas to beautiful harmony. In time philosophy always follows after religion. After a certain wealth of verities and errors had existence in consciousness, reason seized upon them to criticise, sift and construct organic systems. In the ancient treasures of man's religion, Bible or Koran, Vedas of Zendavesta, traditional or documental, Aryan or Semite, or rather all of them, there is laid down a vast amount of finished truth, in the most childlike form, without any attempt at formal reasoning, poured forth from the mind by spontaneous inspiration. There is evidently more than one method in the mind to arrive at truth, although we now tie ourselves down to the inductive mode of reasoning. Other generations follow other methods.

It is so well established now that the religious element is in the human mind, history can not be ignored, that Mr. Darwin antedates it even down to his faithful dog, whose obedience, watchfulness, attachment, and veneration for his master he calls religion, exactly as he calls the emotional sounds of animals language, or, as I would call this white handkerchief the moon, because both of them reflect rays of light. All this is very sentimental of Mr. Darwin, but it is not true. It is certain that the dog sees his master; that he sees in him anything besides shape, anything superior in quality and causality, is not merely uncertain or improbable, it is impossible, because no animal possesses the power of abstraction, to the extent of separating qualities from material, effects from causes, external from internal attributes. Yet it is at that very point where religion begins, where self-contemplation discovers, or supposes to have discovered, outside of the self, being superior in quality and causality. Whether the savage then calls it ghost, spirit, demon, or God, of which he believes one or a legion; in kind the idea is the same which leads the cultivated man to the knowledge and acknowledgement of one God.

Again, that the dog is attached to his master, is certainly a fact; that he feels veneration, is none. Veneration is a diagonal effect of love and fear, where neither are of a sensual nature. We venerate a person whose mental or moral qualities we love, and whose authority or influence we fear, all of which are abstract qualities, and the dog possesses not that power of abstraction. Yet veneration is the next primary element of religion.

Anyhow, also according to Darwin, the religious element is in man in all stages and phases of his cultural development. Then it is no less certain that spiritual self-consciousness is in man *a priori*, as he could not place outside of himself that which is not in him. Seeing spirit outside of himself, he must first have discovered and contemplated it, conscious or unconscious, in himself, *i. e.*, the spirit must first know its own existence—must be self-conscious, before it can set itself, real or imaginery, outside of itself. That which is no substance at all can not even be imagined. Therefore the most ancient ghosts among all nations, as it is still the case among Chinese and others, are departed souls of human beings.

In religion, therefore, in every phase of development, the mind first recognizes itself as a substantial being, and produces out of itself, by spontaneous inspiration, all the truths and errors of the various religions. Therefore in all religious monuments of history, mind has become permanently objective. It is in them that the mind has stepped outside of itself, and stands photographed before the observer, so that no more evidence of its substantiality should be necessary, especially if we cast a cursory glance also upon philosophy.

It is, indeed, a glorious and majestic exemplary of a being, so small, so weak, so circumscribed in space and time as man is, if he spontaneously breaks through all limits of space and time, and in his consciousness, contemplation, and devotion, rises to the infinite, immense, eternal, and universal, above and beyond all things which the senses perceive, the imagination can depict, or the universe in its outward manifestations can impress; when man by the mere necessity of his nature worships the God he contemplates. The materialist should at least feel induced to acknowledge, there is nothing like it in all the phenomena of this universe.

Greater still, more sublime and more divine than in his religion, man appears in his unbroken chain of philosophy from Job and the author of *Koheloth* down to Spencer and Hartman. The mind having soared through the infinite universe, returns into itself and seeks clearness, transparency and certainty ; carves out new methods of thought, tries, sifts, compares, and contemplates everything to arrive at certainty. The insignificant little man who sits in the corner of a narrow room, quiet, isolated, and speechless, hour after hour, and night after night, before a dim flame, penetrating with his mind's eye heaven and heaven's heaven, the mighty deep of creation's fathomless sea, gazing upon the grand scheme of the universe, watching and listening at the labratory of nature, to the mysteries of existence, the harmony, beauty, and wisdom of the boundless all, seeking and searching the proper formulas, to communicate and to prove all the greatness and glory which his mind has conceived;—yes such a little man with the reflex of the universe in him, one should think must have a mind, something incomparable to what we know by experimental science; for he rises to the dignity of an infinite being in comparison to any and everything in this universe which we do know.

This, however, all philosophers do. They cease to be mortal beings, when the mind is engulfed in the contemplation of the universe. They are no longer in time when they contemplate eternity, no longer on earth when they penetrate endless space, no more perishable individuals when engulphed in eternal Deity, as did prophet, theosophist or philosopher at all times. This ought to convince the materialist that there are minds, as none has ever been able to discover the slightest difference in the organic machine of the greatest thinker and the most humble peasant. But there is mind. Hegel has given us a correct idea of philosophy which is the most wonderful chapter in the records of human deeds. It is vulgarly supposed, one philosophical school upsets what another had built up, and all turns in a sort of vicious circle. This is a mistake. With every onward step philosophy becomes more perfect and its field larger. Each thinker is the heir of all his predecessors. Whatever we know and understand now, is the mental work of previous thinkers, to which we add our own, however little it may be. We correct and increase continually. What was philosophy in Egypt three thousand and more years ago is now in the school-boy's text book and impregnates the air we breathe. And what is now profound philosophy for the select few, will be common property ef all in a thousand or less years hence; for intelligence now travels fast. Hence not merely minds, the mind is philosophical.

Another vulgar error is, that philosophical speculation is all subjective, natural science alone is objective. Yet, if philosophy had not leveled the path, natural science could never have come into existence. Philosophy, what do I say? Gœthe in his morphology sees ahead of natural science to its present height. But this is not the point to be disposed of here. The philosopher of every age is the mere focus, in which the dispersed rays of his generation's intelligence, meet in unity and harmony. None did ever stand very high above his age, and none ever will. This is an acknowledged principle in the philosophy of history. The philosopher comprehends the ideas which are often unconscious in the multitude of his cotemporaries, expresses them intelligibly, unites them consciously to a system, to become a stepping stone to the Genius of History, pressing onward and forward, irresistibly and unceasingly. Therefore there are not only philosophical minds, there is mind.

We can sum up thus : In language and history mind is actualized in countless monuments, each of which, is an actualization of ideas, which have no source outside of human mind. In them, mind is objective in stereotyped deeds, and their systematical unity. In art and science, mind is actualized as inventive intelligence and governing will, apart of, and superior to, all forces known to the naturalist. In religion, mind recognizes, and places itself objectively outside of itself. In philosophy, mind contemplates itself in the universal mind, and inverts also the terms, so that the subjective becomes objective and *vice versa.*

If one can possibly overlook the Logos of Language and the Genius of History, and comprehend not the monumental objectivity of the human mind; if one can go by the mighty achievements of science and art, the control and dominion which man assumes over the earth, its elements and forces, the power of mind which he manifests in his implements and machines, from the plough to the locomotive, steam ship, water works, optical, physical, and mathematical instruments; if in our days of thousand-fold triumph over matter and its forces, one can still doubt the existence of mind, let him try to doubt the mind which has become objective in the religious and ethical monuments of the human family, and which manifests itself perpetually and continually; and if he by some unknown means can do even this, let him try to account for the existence of philosophy without the existence of mind ; or, if you please, let him show sunlight without a sun, or an ocean without water. Without mind, there can be neither language nor history, neither art nor science, neither religion nor philosophy. These things are, and they are in and by man only; therefore there is mind. Our problem is solved, my postulate is established "There is mind." Now I am ready to philosophize.

As we shall philosophize inductively, let me say here

what induction signifies, or rather let us hear Victor Cousin on this point. He says:

"Call to mind by what processes and upon what conditions we obtain a law in the physical order. When a phenomenon presents itself with such a character in such circumstance, and when, the circumstance changing, the character of the phenomenon changes also, it follows that this character is not a law of the phenomenon; for this phenomenon can still appear, even when this character no longer exists. But if this phenomenon appears with the same character in a succession of numerous and diverse cases, and even in all the cases that fall under the observation, we hence conclude that this character does not pertain to such or such a circumstance, but to the existence itself of the phenomenon. Such is the process which gives to the physical philosopher and to the naturalist what is called a law. When a law has been thus obtained by observation, that is, by the comparison of a great number of particular cases, the mind in possession of this law transfers it from the past to the future, and predicts that, in all the analogous circumstances that can take place, the same phenomenon will be produced with the same character. This prediction is induction: induction has for a necessary condition a supposition, that of the constancy of nature; for leave out this supposition, admit that nature does not resemble herself, and the night does not guarantee the coming day, the future eludes foresight, and there no longer exists anything but arbitrary chance: all induction is impossible. The supposition of the constancy of nature is the necessary condition of induction; but this condition being granted, induction, resting upon sufficient observation, has all its force."

LECTURE VI.

HOMO-BRUTALISM REVIEWED.

LADIES AND GENTLEMEN,—Some men of learning and genius like Messrs. Vogt, Haeckel, Moleschott, Huxley, Darwin, Buechner and others, have imposed a hypothesis on science, which reduces man, on the scale of organic beings, to an ape, casually and mechanically improved, or some similar animal, no longer extant as a living organism or dead fossil, *i. e.* an imagined animal, one constructed by phantasy on the strength of induction, legitimate, or illegitimate, is supposed to have been the ancestor of man, and several kinds of apes. The monkeys not having improved themselves from casual and mechanical causes unknown, are still irredeemable monkeys. Some of them, however, having casually and mechanically gone through a series of improvements and changes, then by laws of inheritance and correlation have become human beings, and with them the history of mankind begins. Permit me to call this main hypothesis *Homo-Brutalism*, as it has hitherto been given no name at all.

On the whole, this hypothesis is not based upon acknowledged facts; it rests upon an attempt of explaining the genesis of organic beings in a manner more agreeable to our understanding at the present altitude of natural science. It is altogether ingenious, and dependant upon supposed facts which may or may not turn up. Then again the main hypothesis rests upon a number of auxiliary hypotheses, such as the combat for existence, sexual selection and law of correlation, each of which is without the least foundation in acknowledged and undisputed fact; so that one must believe in a long biological creed of numerous hypothetical articles, in order to be an approved Darwinist. It appears to me, the whole theory of Darwinian transmutation is poetical, though beautiful still very uncertain. I discuss this point elsewhere. But in regard to the genesis of man, the theory is an entire failure, although repropped by Haeckel in a voluminous attempt of logical force. Haeckel is the logician and Huxley the scientist of that school.

Poor man! First the priest came with his indistinct notions of religion, or his cunning devices to establish and enforce his authority, and now science with a false face steps in, to rob man of his dignity, to place him many degrees below the dumb idol or among the beasts of the field, and to subject all to iron, relentless, cold, dead, and unreasoning Fate, casualty, dead mechanism. Freedom and reason were set aside by the priest and man was made a helpless tool in the hands of powers beyond his control, a soulless slave of his priest, who was himself the tool of an idol or demon under the relentless absolutism of cold, dead, and iron Fate. This piece of heartless stupidity was found so convenient an instrument of government, to oppress the masses and frighten them to blind obedience and groanless suffering, that rulers in common with priests, where they were not themselves the rulers, seized upon the terrifying falsehood and imposed it by all means at their command, until the human family was fairly divided into slaves and taskmasters. In Egypt as in India, in Greece as in ·Rome, with all the boasted civilization, two.thirds of all men were slaves or Pariahs, the living chattles of cunning and violent men; because the consciousness of man's dignity and pre-eminence was deadened, and blind Fate terrified him.

Through the channel of Rome with her pernicious policy, that piece of dogmatic poison was inherited by modern nations in the form of original sin and universal depravity, and a scheme of salvation based upon this error ; the same enemy to freedom and intelligence, the same nightmare to self-consciousness as the ancient fatalism. Man must be corrupt, depraved, wicked, abject, helpless, forlorn, so that the priest can step in with his self-fabricated god or gods, and his dogmatic dodges, to cheat the devil out of the ignorant and deluded soul, kneeling blind and spell-bound before the terror stricken idols of his bewildered imagination. True, the priest is also under the curse of the original sin and universal depravity; but he invents dogmatic subterfuges to prove conclusively, that he is not he; he is another fellow in the gown and another again outside thereof; that human reason, is not human reason, it is the devil's tricks; and man's moral feelings are not moral at all, unless he believes the priest's well-arranged hocus-pocus. In order that none publish the fraud, thousands of innocent fellows, rational thinkers, idealists, enthusiasts, and philanthropists, men, women, and childreen were slaughtered, burnt at the pyre, driven to misery and despair, or incarcerated in subterranean holes, by the thousands, yea, by the tens of thousands; philosophy and science, popular enlightenment and common education were put under the ban, and the sword of worldly power executed Satan's terrible decrees.

After men had been for centuries so thoroughly robbed of every consciousness of human dignity and pre-eminence, like a pack of frightened sheep, there stepped in the emperor, the king, the prince, the ruler, the nobility, all like the priest by the grace of God, and contracted a co-partnership with the successful priesthood, to fleece the sheep, to grow fat on the mutton, to trample under their feet the unpromising lambkin; to degrade, brutalize and enslave God's own image. Helpless man, without the free use of his reason, without reliance in his conscience, without consciousness of his dignity and pre-eminence, became a slave with body and soul.

In spite, however, of all violence, wickedness, and cunningness, human nature could not be extinguished. Ever since Copernicus, Keppler, and Galileo gave us an idea of space, the priest's miniature gods became very small and insignificant, merely local magistrates, and the devil with his hell and ministering demons could be located no longer. Then came Lord Bacon, and the Humanists, Descartes, Spinoza, Locke, and Leibnitz, followed by a host of free and independent thinkers, defied priest and king in the name of soverign truth, and the morning dawned. Men were roused to a recognition of their own dignity and pre-eminence, and the revolutions came, in the Netherlands against bloody Spain, in Germany by downtrodden peasants, in England under Cromwell and the Ironsides, then in this country, in France, everywhere, so that we still live in the midst of revolutions, which will not end before man has gained his freedom and independence, the last crown, throne, and scepter shall be broken, the last monarch and the last priest of darkness shall have abjured their wicked occupations, man shall be re-instated in his rights, in the full consciousness of his dignity and pre-eminence as a man, reason, conscience, and freedom shall reign universally and forever. PROUD, proud I say, down with that abject humility, proud man must be made, in order to become virtuous and wise in due self-respect. The old slavery, contrition and creeping obedience must be banished out of him, to be a man again.

So it came that on the benign fountain of philosophy

and science, man began to recover. In the midst of uncounted millions of stupified and terrified people, who can not exist without a potentate and a priest—who must be fleeced, ruled, dandled, or whipped—there arose a powerful intelligence, a self-conscious and enlightened element. It rose in broad daylight to proclaim man's emancipation from all authorities, his right to be free, and his duty to guard human dignity against all offenses. Man began to recognize himself and his fellow-man again in their true dignity and pre-eminence, and a better future dawned. But alas! there comes false-faced science with its ventursome hypotheses, the modern diseases of materialism and Darwinism, committing the same errors over again, places blind and irrational Fate on the throne of the God of wisdom and love, pushes man back among the irrational brutes, deprives him of his dignity and pre-eminence, degrades, terrifies, and bewilders him. It is the same curse as ever, the same defiance of reason and philanthropy as heretofore, the same retrogressive movement to bring misery on the human family.

Look especially upon the Darwinian hypothesis. Man is an improved beast. His religion, ethics, and æsthetics, his domestic and social virtues, his intelligence and wisdom, it is all brutal, only that some men have a little more of it than some brutes. Then the speculative scientist steps in and proves to you that it must be so; for there are the ant, the spider, the bee, and the beaver, which do things wonderfully wise; and here are the dog, the horse, the elephant, and the wise sheep, which are both moral and religious. The bumble-bee philosophizes, and the rooster studies æsthetics. All your birds, chickens, geese, and turkeys practice æsthetics, when they fall in love or pine away in unheeded affections, as you may hear in the beautiful cadences of the geese in my neighborhood. There are in Africa some monkeys whose noses are like those of some men, others who have the same teeth as made by our dentists, and others again walk far better erect than any drilled bear or dog. Some of them have beards—mark well, BEARDS—not made out of other people's hair or hemp, but natural beards, long and of various colors; not like the beard of the he-goat, but like man's, grown by the æsthetical exertions of monkeys in love with hard-hearted monkey dames. Therefore, you see, the conclusion is irresistible; therefore all those monkeys and man must be the descendants of one and the same beast, of whose existence we have no knowledge; and that beast was the offspring of another and lower beast, and that again of another, and so on and on, down to the original dirt upon which the sun shone for the first time. There in that original dirt you may discover the history of all living creatures, all the morals, intelligence, and languages of man. But the spectacles must be correct and made in the Darwinian factory. Here is your Darwinism in brief.

In a moral point of view the Darwinian hypothesis on the descent of man is the most pernicious that could be possibly advanced, not only because it robs man of his dignity and the consciousness of pre-eminence, which is the coffin to all virtue, but chiefly because it presents all nature as a battle-ground, a perpetual warfare of each against all in the combat for existence, and represents the victors as those worthy of existence, and the vanquished ripe for destruction. So might is right, the cardinal sin is to be the weekest party. If this is nature's law, and man is an improved beast, then war to the knife, perpetual war of each against all, is also human law, and peace in any shape is illegitimate and unnatural. Therefore in all cases of expulsion, assassination or slaughter, among individuals or nations, the vanquished party was doomed in advance, by a law of nature; and the victors having enforced the laws of nature are neither culpable nor responsible for their deeds. The British Parliament is not ready, I opine, to endorse this doctrine. The case is aggravated by the auxiliary hypothesis of sexual selection. If the most careful sexual selection makes the most perfect human beings, then the potentates and nobility of the Old World have a twofold right to their claim of superiority and their title to govern others, and we poor and deluded democrats, who claim equality of rights for all, are in error; for the aristocrats of the Old World are the victors, or their descendants, by the most careful sexual selection, and we plebeians are sons of our mothers and fathers, who were ordinary mortals. So with ancient materialism and fatalism, we are led back to the ancient factions and clans of society with all the misery of that system; inalienable and inborn rights, equality, liberty and the pursuit of happiness, are mere terms of a compact, and none a truth *per se*; the most improved felons are the lords of land and sea; and the other trash which has to be extinguished any how, is merely tolerated for the lords' special accommodation. It appears to me that Darwinism is tolerated in Europe, because it props the aristocracy. This point deserves much more consideration than I can give it in this lecture, as I do not mean to review the hypothesis from a moral standpoint; I intend to place fact against fact, and will begin at once.

In the first place the Darwinists ought to prove the unity of the human race, to render it plausible that the monkey changed into an Ethiopian, the Ethiopian into a Mongolian, and he into a Caucasian. The unity or diversity of the human family is no settled question in science. In England, it is true, the Doctors Prichard and Latham maintained the unity of the human family, hence the descent of all human varieties from one pair of human beings. But in America the contrary opinion has been advanced and well defended by Dr. Morton, Prof. Agassiz, the doctors W. Usher and J. C. Nott, Prof. S. H. Patterson and other prominent scientists. They maintain the diversity of the human family, consequently the descent of the various races from different first parents. In Germany also much has been written and nothing established about this point; so that F. L. Lange steps conveniently across this stumbling block with the authoritative remark that it is immaterial. So it is in ethics and politics, but not in the theory of evolution; for here are plain facts in direct conflict with the Darwinian hypothesis.

The English doctors, if we admit all their evidence and arguments, prove no more than the probability that outer influences may have changed the types of men to what they now are. The fact itself is not established. But there is the anatomical difference in the structure of the head and the texture of the hair, then the difference of color pointing to chemical differences, and above all the ethnological differences in the sum of inventions, language, and civilization, so marked and decisive that the unity of the human race can be maintained by conclusive, scientific evidence only, which neither Mr. Darwin nor his followers advance.

Reference to the Bible will not save the hypothesis. True, the author of Genesis stood so much nearer to the cradle of humanity than we do, and ought to have known more than we of man's origin; still, we have no proof in hand of his infallibility on this point, unless we start out with the belief in revelation. In this case, however, the Darwinian hypothesis falls of itself, as regards the descent of man.

In my opinion, the Bible does not teach the unity of the human race, as I have already advanced in 1854 in my History, (Vol. 1. p. 42), there are not only the sons of Elohim and the daughters of Adam whose origin is doubtful; but also the *Nephilim, Rephaim, Enakim, Horim, Samsumim, Aimim* and several other tribes mentioned in the Bible, who were no descendants of either Adam or Noah.

The hypothesis that the three races, Caucasian, Mongolian and Ethiopian, are descendants of the three sons of Noah, Shem, Ham and Japheth, is utterly false, as the genealogical tables prove. In the case of Ham, the supposed ancestor of the Ethiopians, we know that the Egyptians, Phœnicians and Canaanites were his descendants, and they were all white, so white indeed, that King Solomon married a daughter of Pharoah, King Abab espoused the fair princess of Tyre, and the Hebrews had Canaanitish wives as late as the days of Ezra, although the daughters of Israel were always fair and beautiful, as the great Rabbi Johanan Ben Saccai testifies. There is no doubt in my mind that the author of Genesis knows of the Caucasian race only. His Adam and Noah are the fathers of the Caucasians; his Paradise and Deluge must be located in Southern Asia. True, there are Ethiopian countenances on the Egyptian Pyramids, but they must not necessarily have been there in the time of Moses. The word *Kushi*, translated "Ethiopian," refers to Caucasian Arabs, as is evident from Numbers xii, 1, and II Chronicles xiv, 7 to 14. Very late in Jewish History (Jeremiah xiii, 23) the name *Kushi* is given to a man of another color.

The unity of the human race is not established in science or the Bible. There is no evidence on record that a permanent and lasting transition from race to race can be effected. The last fossil man found, is a Paleolithic skeleton, discovered in the caverns of Metone, in Italy, and is about the same as a modern Caucasian, six feet high, no trace of an ape, and with a skull somewhat inferior to that of Mr. Darwin s. But there are now a number of inferior skulls no human frames; so at that time superior men may have lived simultaneously with that man of Mentone.

It must be remarked here, that all the human fossils found hitherto, those of Cro-Magnon and Hohenfels included, together with all the discoveries of Abbe Burgeois and Tardy, and the learned expositions of Lartet, Mortillet and Warsae, do not prove that those human beings did live in Europe prior to the early period of the Assyrian empire; or that the Glacial time together with the troglodite men and beasts was closed in Europe or America north of the Ohio and Potomac rivers, while there was a high civilization in Asia and Egypt; or that any but the Caucasian ever existed in Europe; or that the human form and construction, head included, underwent any considerable change. We have now Pathegonians and

Esquimaux, Laplanders and the mountaineers of Caucasia, and in all localities between these extremes, we find men of the most diverse construction of skulls. The same precisely is the case with the implements. Stone, bronze and iron implements may have been in use simultaneously in various parts of the world, and I have no doubt they were; as is the case now in many particulars. Professor Fraas himself proves by traditions from antiquity and the European Middle Ages, the existing knowledge from the troglodite period, the stone age, and the glacial time. So there is no fact in existence to prove either the transition from race to race, or any improvement or change of the human frame.

If the races of the human family are permanent, and the proof thereof is as old as history, then the Darwinists are entitled to only one hypothesis in this relation, viz: one class of monkeys transformed themselves into one or more Caucrsian Adams and Eves, others into Mongolians, ann again others into Ethiopians. As we are best acquainted with the Caucasian race we will investigate chiefly, without neglecting the other races entirely, whether or not sufficient points of similiarity between man and monkey offer, to establish the fact of a common ancestry; or if sufficient points of dissimiliarity exist to deny the allegation. I will say in advance, however, that to me, man, of course woman included, is too dear a creature, to be identified with or compared to any sublunar being. Man is the most beautiful and most perfect work of nature. Sun, moon, stars, rainbow and flowers compare not in beauty to the human countenance. There is nothing as lovely, tender and impressive as man's face, nothing more wonderful than his brilliant eye, more heavenlike than his voice in song and speech, more sublime than a firm moral character, or more divine than a man contemplating God and eternity. All similes fail, all comparisons are false; man stands alone and incomparable on this earth. But we deal in a scientific question, will and must handle it in the scientific method.

LECTURE VI.

HOMO-BRUTALISM—REVIEWED ANATOMICALLY

Ladies and Gentlemen:—Permit me to state that I admire Mr. Darwin as an eminent biologist, whose hypotheses deserve a careful consideration. He displays more originality of thought in his particular branch than many prominent men, and his research is vast and wonderful. Men like Darwin are very rare, few and far apart. He deserves our admiration. His main hypothesis, however, to account for the origin of species, together with the auxiliary hypotheses, appears to me not established in fact, and insufficient to account for the genesis of organisms. I furthermore think, that the German disciples and admirers morally pressed him to write his Descent of Man, which is the most unscientific book he did write.

Homo-Brutalism in its modern garb, is much older than Darwin's book. It was first advanced by the zoologist Carl Vogt in a book which appeared in 1863. Mr. Haeckel, the German adviser of Mr. Huxley, was the man who gave the matter a strictly scientific and logical form, basing upon the Darwinian theory of evolution, or rather mechanical transmutation. This pressed Mr. Darwin, to come forward with the last result of the hypothesis, attempting to establish the descendency of man from some unknown brutal ancestor, the progenitor of the anthropomorphous apes, especially the Gorilla, Ourang, Chimpanzee and Gibbon, which bear, structural resemblances to man; because, as Mr. Darwin says, "As man agrees with them not only in all those characters which he possesses in common with the Catarhine group, but in other peculiar characters, such as the absence of a tail and callosities, and in general appearance, we may infer that some ancient member of the anthropomorphous sub-group gave birth to man" (Descent of Man, Vol. 1 p. 189.)

Man's resemblance to the Catarhine monkeys is based chiefly upon his nostrils, jaws, and teeth,.and this is about all he has in common with them, so that we might justly infer that man in smelling and grinding the food resembles those monkeys. All other inferences are illegitimate. Man's resemblance to the anthropomorphous apes consists of the general appearance, which as a general thing amounts to very little, and the absence of tail and callosities. If, however, the absence of any member or phenomenon is a good criterion of common genealogy, then man may just as well be considered of common descent with the lion or cat, for both of them wear mustaches, have neither tusks nor trunks, and there are white cats with blue eyes; only that our white beauties with blue eyes are not deaf, and cats of that kind usually are. But this wonderful change may have been brought about by sexual selection, in the course of a few millions of years, of course, since the Tertitary Age, as Mr. Haeckel wants it. Any how it is for the first time in science, that nonenity is considered an adequate criterion, to establish a fact.

Some of the ancients were of the opinion, that those anthropomorphous apes were accursed men, fallen men, men punished for their misdeeds, like King Nebuchadnezzar; and there is as much sense in this as in the other hypothesis. If those apes bear a stronger resemblance to man than to the lower monkeys, as Mr. Huxley maintains, I know not on what ground, and our sober experience teaches, that man may be brutalized, while brutes can not be humanized; well, then, it is much more scientific to maintain that those apes are deterioated Ethiopians, than to advance that the Australian aborigene is an improved ape. It could be quite well supposed, that in prehistoric ages, at a time probably when Australia was connected with Asia, there was no communication between the tribes who lived far apart on account of the combat for existence; individuals expelled from their tribes on account of misdeeds, or losing their way in unbroken forests, went like Cain to the land of Nod, straggled far away, became low savages at this or that point, and finally apelike beings at other points. Huxley admits that the Australians are of Egyptain origin; hence he must admit deterioration in fact. If the proud race of *Mitzraim* could become savage and crippled Australians, why not also baboons? If on the one hand it is admitted that the monkey's hands could change gradually to human feet, and the hairy, rough and dark skin of the ape could be tanned and bleached to the soft and white skin of the Caucasian, why should not human feet, by climbing be changed into hands, and the naked body exposed to inimical elements, not become rough, dark, and hairy? Those who did not succeed in that adaption, we would say with Mr. Darwin, died out, and the changed individuals survived. All the other hypotheses of Mr. Darwin are applicable in this case much better than their opposite.

The hypothesis of the ancients, I think is even preferable to Mr. Darwin's, because it rests upon experienced facts, and Mr. Darwin's does not. It has its proof even in embryology. The human embryo at a certain status is hairy, but this condition is overcome by the progressive development of the human being. If a state is overcome by the progressive development in the embryo, it might re-appear by the retrogression of the being to that lower condition. If the Darwinian would ask, why did man deteriorate to an anthropomorphous and not to another animal, I could reply for the ancients; because like Vogt, Haeckel, Huxley, Darwin and the others, those straggling Ethiopians met among other animals also the Catarhine monkeys and mistook them for something akin to human beings, anyhow more sociable, less ferocious and more docile than other animals; therefore they associated with them, then aped them, and at last became like them, as analogous facts abundantly prove. If the Darwinian ask furthermore what is gained by the hypothesis of the ancients, I could answer for them a good deal; it saves the dignity of man, and might encourage the mission societies to send their pious and zealous missionaries to the poor, neglected and lost apes, and quench the philanthropic thirst of good natured matrons. Is this nothing? Ask our enthusiastic friends, whether this is not a great deal. Then I would turn upon the Darwinian and ask him, what is gained by your hypothesis? Does it explain one trait of human character or one feature of his organism? Is it of any earthly use to the physician, scientist, statesman, politician, law maker, ruler historian or philosopher? Evidently not, none can turn it to any practical purpose. It only degrades man, and gives him nothing in return.

So, I believe, most all Darwinian hypotheses could be led *ad absurdum*, especially those concerning the Descent of Man, which present a momentary aberration of the human mind, a sporadic and epidemic disease of an overloaded age, as was at its respective time alchemy, astrology, phrenology, and exploded exorcism. It is hardly necessary now, to argue against the Darwinian hypothesis on the descent of man, as little is left of it which European thinkers have not refuted. From our standpoint, the diversity of the human family, comparing the Caucasian man to the anthropomorphous ape, the dissemblance is so striking, that a common genealogy is impossible. Let us cast a glance upon anatomy first.

None of the defenders of homo-brutalism will admit to be so ignorant of anatomy, that he could not distinguish *prima vista*, between any human bone or muscle and the corresponding bone or muscle of an ape. The same precisely is the case with the texture of skin and hair, and their color. Evidently we have before us in each case another combination of cells different in structure, constituents and proportions. We deal here in chemical, consequently substantial differences, realized in different morphotic structures, which no sensible man can begin to account for, except by dissimilar differentiations of the vital force. There is no other cause known. Then the difference between man and ape in morphology is as marked and decisive as that of a deer and an oak.

But the anatomic dissemblances are also marked and decisive. Man has two hands and two feet, to begin with the locomotive organs, and the monkey has four hands, used as feet, to crawl, leap, or climb. Mr. Darwin tells us, during the millions of years, two of the monkey's hands, by application and inheritance, were changed to human feet. This might just as well have been accomplished, as the dark rough and hairy skin of the ape could be transformed into the soft, smooth, and white skin of the Caucasian; or as well as the dull eye of the baboon could be improved to the large, lustrous and expressive eye of man; or the monkey skull could be proportioned and rounded to a human head. Yes, I would reply, one is as possible as the other. The question in this case, from the Darwinian standpoint, is, why should the man ape change two of his hands to mere feet? Sexual selection had nothing to do with it; for no monkey dame could have possibly thought of a bi-handed or bi-footed lover, whose prehensile and defensive powers were so much decreased. With four hands one can sieze better than with two. In self-defense or labor, four hands will do better than two; hence natural selection and the combat for existence had nothing to do with the wanton change. The ape with four hands and prehensile tail runs, leaps, climbs and defends himself better than a two handed and unarmed man can. Hence there was no gain, there was a great loss in the change to the animal; why then should it have attempted such a deplorable change? Here Mr. Darwin's teleology fails, if he resorts not to the very unlikely hypothesis, that the man-ape felt the necessity of assuming an erect posture, which is the most marked dissemblance of man and beast. Let us investigate this point.

The erect posture and bipedal walk of man is one of his characteristics falling in the eye of the most cursory observer. The whole character of a man finds expression in his posture and gait. His feelings, emotions, thoughts, intentions and resolutions are demonstrated in the positions of his body and the peculiarity of his steps; so that both are peculiarly human. This posture and gait are made possible by the anatomical structure of his bones and muscles. Without this pelvis, this spinal column, this clavicle, scapula, and sternum, with their peculiar muscles and nerves, upright posture is unnatural and bipedal walk impossible as a rule. The dog, bear, or ape may be drilled to assume it, but it is a perpetual strain and violence on them. Man only is constructed to look heavenward, onward, and forward. Mr. Vogt with all his partiality for the ape, nevertheless admits, that the structure of man differs entirely from the ape, and man only is built to walk erect. This is also the last word of Haeckel and Huxley on this point, so that the latter admits, that links in the chain of creatures between man and ape are certainly missing. All rational zoologists admit that the structure of the rump, and not the locomotive organs decides the character of an organic being. In the rump, however, there exists not as much resemblance between man and ape as between the lion and opossum, or the deer and the rat. If Mr. Darwin tells me, that now the structure of man makes the upright posture necessary and natural, but millions of years ago it was otherwise, I must ask why? how can you possibly know it? If it is, because the dog, bear, or ape can be taught to assume exceptionally an erect posture, you can not change his bones and muscles to give it permanency; how do you know it could at all be done at any time? and if you have no fact to show the bare possibility, are no prophet, and no son of a prophet, what right have you to advance a hypothesis in science, which has no foundation in fact and explains no phenomenon?

Moreover, I would ask Mr. Darwin, why should the man-ape ever have attempted to walk erect, stretch, strain, disjoint, and dislocate bones and muscles, which must have been quite painful to that creature, merely to assume a position so unnatural to him? He could not possibly anticipate that by this exertion his whole frame will undergo a revolution to make of him a man and a Caucasian, nor could he care for it; yet the fact is universally admitted, that the human head, brain, countenance, the entire man is as he is, on account of his erect posture.

In the combat of existence the man-ape could only injure himself by the tormenting experiment, which must have made him so much more helpless and defenseless, as it does to-day the dog, bear, or ape, in that unnatural position. Sexual selection had certainly nothing to do with it; for the ape-dame could not possibly be more partial to a helpless admirer who made a caricature of himself than to one of her own kind and taste. Mr. Darwin has not advanced one holding point, and I can guess none, to prove the mere probability that man ever was a four-handed, creeping ape, or that the ape could chemically and morphotically change his entire frame for that of man; hence as far as anatomy is concerned, the hypothesis is groundless and childish.

Still, if there be one within hearing distance to doubt this point, let him be reminded that man has a larynx in his throat by which he is enabled to utter articulate speech and human song; yes, a larynx, with its five cartilaginous pieces, which no animal has. Therefore man alone speaks articulate language and sings human songs which no animal can do. The animal having no ideas to express, has no use for a larynx, therefore it has none. Man is a man because he can speak articulate language and sing human song. He must have words to remember, abstract, reason, judge, establish principles, laws, science, philosophy, religion, ethics, æsthetics, all that is peculiarly human. Without speech society with all its blessings, civilization with all its advantages, man in his present condition are impossible. Yet without these instruments of speech, articulate words could not be uttered. Here Mr. Darwin's difficulty is simply insurmountable. Did the man-ape manufacture his larynx in order to be enabled to speak articulate sounds, of which he had no idea? Can so important an organ, upon which the entire fate of humanity depends, be produced by an animal? Where is the analogy, the parallel case? Has man, or has any animal, by any exertion ever succeeded in producing such an important instrument in his body? Experience answers emphatically, no. Common sense can only ridicule the idea, that without any imaginable cause an animal should entertain the notion of producing articulate speech. Our horses, dogs, cows, and other domestic animals, especially the Arab's camel, have associated with man thousands of years, still none have acquired a larnyx in his throat. He can not be man without articulate speech. No animal speaks and none has a larnyx, consequently man must have appeared on this earth with these organs of speech, the cause of speech in his mind and its instruments in his body. Therefore, if it were for no other reason, man could never have been an ape or any other animal.

But here we step outside of anatomy upon the field of psychology, and I do not wish to confuse my hearers. Therefore I must leave the psychological argument for our next lecture, and stop here. You see the single points of dissemblance in anatomy are not supposed to constitute fully the dissemblance of man and ape. Take them altogether, and they do establish the point. We have before us in man an entirely anomalous structure of chemical and morphotic peculiarity. We have before us a bipedal, erect, and speaking being, with hands which Aristotle called the instrument of instruments, an external appearance different from all animals, head, eye, and countenance peculiar to themselves only, which none can rationally explain except by another cause; another cause must be at work in the construction of man, another at the construction of animals.

It is various differentation of vital force. Yet, if there were no structural dissemblances between man and ape, if man were completely ape-like in his body; his mind, his intelligence, his moral feelings and his works would fully distinguish him and entitle him to the consciousness that man is a man for all that, and nothing can be compared to him. We have no confreres among the animals. They can not think with us, hence they can not feel with us. But we discuss this point in our next lecture.

LECTURE VIII.

HOMO-BRUTALISM—REVIEWED PSYCHOLOGICALLY.

Ladies and Gentlemen:—It appears to me, the more conclusively zoologists and somatologists prove the identity of human and animal organisms, the more thoroughly they prove the existence and substantiality of human mind as the efficient cause of the bodily organism. For there are capacities, abilities, feelings, and aspirations in man, to which the animal offers no more analogy than the squeak of a mouse to a symphony of Beethoven; and these distinguishing qualities of man are no less facts in science than those revealed by telescope or microscope, experience, or experiment, chemist or anatomist. If they depend on the organism, why are they not in all organisms as well as in man's? Or why not at least in those which are so similar to man, as Haeckel and Darwin maintain? And yet the psychical dissemblance of man and beast is so conspicuous and self-evident, that the most zealous apostles of homo-brutalism can not help confessing the utter incomparableness of man and brute. If we would know only this one point, that those doctors dissect, describe, delineate, dissolve, and classify animals, which no animal since the days of old grandfather Adam has thought of doing, it would suffice to establish the utter psychical dissemblance of man and beast; for it proves that man reasons and the brute does not.

It appears to me, that there are two fundamental errors in the psychology of homo-brutalism. The first error is this. The advocates of that theory point out some isolated traits of human intelligence or feeling, disconnected with the general character of man, as prejudiced sectarians expound Bible passages; and then attempt to show that something similar is manifested by this or that animal, especially of the lowest orders, such as the bee, ant, or spider. Having discovered some similiarities of this kind in various animals, one trait here and another there, they jump to the conclusion of semblance between all men and all beasts.

In every alleged fact of this kind, the question recurs, is that attribute observed in the animal really there, or is it imposed on it by the interested observer. This question well answered, in every particular case, that such humanlike attributes are indeed discerned among lower animals, then on the general principle of evolution, one must naturally suppose, those humanlike traits of intelligence or feeling will increase in number and quality as you rise in the progressive scale of organism, and approach man. But no, the bee, ant, spider, and other little creatures evince more intelligence than the dog, horse, elephant or ape. Where then is their psychical line of descendency up to man? There is none. Where is the law upon which to establish succession? There is none. Well then, what entitles anybody to a theory of psychical evolution? As the matter stands now, it is easier to establish the common descent of man, with the bee, ant, or spider, from one brutal ancestry than to support successfully the similar hypothesis in regard to man and the anthropomorphous ape.

Again isolated traits of humanlike intelligence or feeling in various animals, however apparent, form no criterion of semblance; for the human mind which makes his character, is indivisible. It consists not of this or that special trait without all the others belonging thereto. When you say man, you deal in no fractions. When you say human body, you mean all the parts thereof as a unit. When you say human mind, you mean one indivisible being in which all traits of that character are the constituents. You can mean only one luminary when you say sun; and all the isolated rays of light you may contemplate, have no resemblance to the sun. A thing, part man and part beast is an anomaly, like a thing which is part sun and part moon. We can neither imagine nor think it, nature offers no analogy to it. One humanlike trait here and another there scattered all over the animal kingdom, afford no better foundation to Darwin's hypothesis on the descent of man, than my hypothesis, if I should ever venture it, that the sun evolved from the stars, would afford, because each star sends us some rays of light which resemble rays from the sun.

If there was in existence any creature of structural and psychical resemblance with man and beast, or such a creature was barely imaginable or thinkable, the Darwinian hypothesis might deserve some credence. But as the matter really stands, patching together bones, muscles, organs, traits of character, intelligence, feelings, and gestures from a thousand different sources, and constituting thereof an anomaly, to which nature offers no analogy, and then base upon this patchwork of imagination the useless and aimless hypothesis of man's descent from an ape, in my opinion, is simply absurd and fantastic.

The second error in the psychology of homo-brutalism is this. Its advocates look upon mind by the category of quantity instead of quality. They represent the case, as if there was a grain of mind in this animal, two grains in that, three or four in the next. Then as you rise in the scale of evolution the quantity of mind increases, till you reach man who has several pounds of it; that is to say, those who have it. The savage has only one pound of mind, probably, Isaac Newton may have had ten, and we learned doctors of this decade, who know so much more than all our predecessors, must have each a twenty-five pounder of a mind. We must have feelings as thick as a beam, and thoughts of the specific gravity at least of gold, with a fine prospect ahead of infinite growth. Unfortunately neither Moses nor Aristotle has been duplicated in history, and two thousand years ago the children of Jerusalem like our own this day, commenced going to school at the age of six; so that inheritance did not do us much good.

With the materialist, of course, quantity is the main category. In Darwinism, many brutal minds, if such a thing exists, make one human mind, which is a compound of bee mind, ant, and spider mind, fox mind, dog mind, oppossum mind, ape mind, etc., something like the broth in the kettle of Macbeth's witches.

Mind must be contemplated under the category of quality. Red is not blue, and yellow is not purple, although they are colors all of them. A candle light is no gasflame, an electric flash is no sunshine, although it is all light anyhow. So no animal mind bears the least semblance to any human mind, nor can all the millions of brutal spirits in the aggregate make one human mind, as little indeed, as all oceans can be set in place of one moon. One thing can not be another, which is of other qualities, as other qualities are manifestations of another force which is the thing's substance. You can not speak of more or less mind; you can only speak of another mind. Therefore, if the Darwinian evolution of organisms could be established, evolution of mind is no less impossible;

and it is infinitely strange, that reasoners should not detect *prima vista* these two fundamental errors.

Look upon the matter from the empirical side, and you arrive at the same result precisely. The most superficial psychologist must be able to discover the following strongly marked distinctions of man and beast:

All the instincts and manifestations of the animal are resultants from the principle of preservation, self-preservation, and preservation of the race. This principle is the animal's center, toward which all its functions and exertions tend, from its birth to its death. If let alone to its instincts, it does nothing else. It divides its time in periods of feeding, propagation, rest, and what belongs immediately to either. It manifests no other wants, desires, wishes, hopes, or fears. All observation of animal nature has not led outside of this periphery; so that all biologists, Mr. Darwin included, must admit this universal criterion of animal nature. In exact harmony with this principle, is also the animal's mental capacity. It knows no more, nor does it possess any impulse or capacity to know more, than the objects connected directly with its preservation. All observation of animal dexterity has not revealed one fact leading beyond this narrow limit. Therefore we may lay down as a fact, animal life is entirely subjective, without the power of ideality or objectivity.

The lowest instincts of man, those which he continually seeks to modify, to check, and to control by his moral-intellectual force and its ideals, are the resultants of the self-same instinct of preservation, self-preservation and preservation of the race. The combat of this instinct and its resultants on the one side, and the ideals of its intellectual, moral, aesthetical, and religious nature, on the other side, is incessant and perpetual. True humanity begins with the victories of the latter and the submission of the former. In strict harmony therewith is also man's power of cognition, which extends to all objects, real or ideal, their qualities and the abstractions thereof. Hence human life is subjective objective, with the power of ideality and objectivity; or in other words, human nature begins there, where animal nature has reached its highest and last function; man begins where the animal ceases; hence, again, human nature bears no resemblance whatever to animal nature.

This is not the case with the savage, says the Darwinist, nor with the brutalized persons in civilized society.— We say, to a certain extent it is. Few if any human beings are so savage, that they have no moral and religious ideas at all; having any, however crude, the nature, combat, and results are the same in kind as with the man of higher and more ideals.

Besides, if all our ancestors were savages at one time, they must have evidently had in themselves that moral, intellectual force and ideality, which enabled and compelled them to rise above their lower instincts, or else they could not possibly have done it. Having that force and ideality in them, they were no more like animals than the living germ is like the grain of sand, although identical in shape and quantity. Those persons in civilized society who live a merely brutal life, only prove man's freedom to go as far as suicide, which no animal can do; while the others prove, that human nature actually begins, where animal nature ceases. If only one among a thousand would prove this, it would not alter the case; it would still prove that such is human nature.

But, says the Darwinist, perhaps the animal also might be brought up to that higher state of life, as the dog has learned obedience and veneration, the horse feels an attachment to its rider, the cat flatters the kind mistress of the house, the camel listens to its driver's songs, the elephant fights for its human friend, and so on. All Darwinists, we reply, are respectfully requested to admit, that mere probability without underlying facts furnishes no legitimate evidence in science. As far as human knowledge reaches, it is impossible to develop a human mind in any animal. Whatever domestic animals may have learned of man, has been artificially imposed on them. It is not theirs. It is not the fruit of any germ within them. It is mechanical action, mechanically imposed. Send them away from man, and in a short time they re-assume their natural instincts and characters; but with man, his culture is his own. His particular character is the fruit of germs within him. His humanity grows out of his human nature. He is himself the moral, intellectual, æsthetical, and religious being, who may impose some rules and feelings on the animals about him. All the wit of domestic animals proves as little the resemblance of human and animal nature, as artificial hybrids prove the Darwinian origin of species, by a supposed law of mechanical transmutation.

Besides, we have before us proof positive that animal nature can never become human nature. We know the existence and nature of a force by the effects it produces. There is no other criterion to recognize and characterize force. We examine the phenomena and judge the force which produces them. We have before us all which animals have done, and all which men have done. The phenomena show two entirely different forces at work. In man's sphere we have before us the entire work of history, the gigantic structure of civilization, discussed above in the lectures on the objectivity of the human mind. Here is language with all the mental treasures stored away in millions of minds and millions of volumes, all by the means and in the form of articulate sounds. Here is the fathomless ocean of science, all inaccessible and incomprehensible to the animal, because without language it can not form abstract ideas. The animal has no idea of numbers, as I know from repeated experiments. Most of the domestic animals have no steroscopic vision; any white, flat and oval body will do a hen for a nest egg. Most of them can not distinguish colors, and will eat black dyed grass and grain just as well. Most of them have no idea of distance, so that the dog barking at the moon sees her very near and imagines she approaches the dog's own standing point. Without the power of abstraction, the knowledge of numbers, distance, extensions, and colors, to stop here, the animal is incapable of making, classifying and generalizing experiences, or to have any correct knowledge of the things of its cognition. It can have neither a past nor a future, it lives in the present continually. It can remember certain persons and things as totalities, but not the qualities and criteria thereof. Therefore it forgets rapidly the past and the objects seen or heard, possesses none by its criteria, can reproduce none outside of itself, can not combine, reproduce or invent in any form. Mr. Darwin never informs us of the pictures drawn or painted by elephants, statues carved out by monkeys, useful implements or ornaments made by horses or dogs, musical instruments or new compositions made by birds, or the mathematical problems solved by bees, spiders, and ants. The animal can not get outside of itself, because there is nothing in it to be objectivated; man continually objectivates his mind because he has one.

Mr. Darwin's animal æsthetics is manifested in each animal's bodily ornaments; man's æsthetics is objectivated mind in works of art and external ornament. Mr. Darwin's animal morals consist of some unconscious and particular habits of some domestic animals; man's morals begin with the universal principle of respect for the good and the true outside of himself, and the consciousness of freedom to govern his instincts. Mr. Darwin's animal re-religion consists of the dog's brief respect for his master of to-day; and man's religion begins with the cognition of the invisible God, the ideal of all his ideals. Mr. Darwin's animal intelligence consists of a continued sameness of certain mechanical performances; and man's intelligence is manifested in perpetual variations, combinations and inventions. How in the world, men and scholars can compare these entirely different qualities and manifestations, and discover in them any resemblance, is as incomprehensible an absurdity to me, as one, in presence of all the creations of the human mind, and in absence of any creations of the animal mind, can still maintain, both are of the same kind. If it is true that a force must manifest itself, and we know its existence and nature by its resultants; then it must be equally true, that the moral-intellectual force, mind-force, human soul, or whatever it may be called, is in man only, because it manifests itself in human creations of intelligence, morals, æsthetics and religion, it is objectivated ; and it is not in the animal, because it is not manifested in any creations. This force not being in the animal, hence animal nature can never be changed into human nature, as nothing can come out of nothing.

The lowest Australian savage stands as high above and as distinct from the anthropomorphous ape, as Isaac Newton stood above the lowest savage ; for the offspring of that very savage can be educated and humanized, and the ape remains an ape, whatever training you give him; simply because there is human mind in man, and another principle of life in the animal. The Australian aborigine is a deteriorated Ethiopian, thrown back from human habitation, probably by the combat for existence and other causes, brutalized by exclusion and isolation ;as was the case with our Northern Indians cut off from their Southern cognates. Therefore all human beings, if taken care of in their infancy, can be educated and humanized,

I do not mean to say, that I have to advance no more against Mr. Darwin's homo-brutalism ; for the whole application of natural and sexual selections, combat for existence, variability and inheritance, to the development and history of man, is radically erroneous, because secondary causes are made primary ones; and I might discuss every point separately. I mean to say, no more is neccessary in order to upset the hypothesis. It is not based upon any known fact and explains none. It is useless in all departments of human knowledge and practice. It is nugatory to morals, robs man of the consciousness of his dignity and pre-eminence, and brutalizes him. There exists no anatomical resemblance between man and any known animal, as a complete and full organism. There exists no resemblance whatever between human mind, his intelligence, ethics, æsthetics and religion, and the principle of life discoverable in the animal, no resemblance in man's creations and animal doings. I expect to have proved all this, and think no more is necessary for intelligent people, to be convinced of the utter absurdity of homo-brutalism. Therefore I say no more on this topic.

It would be in proper place now, to discuss the origin of species; but we are not prepared to do it, before we have taken a general survey of ontology and biology, in order to ascertain and establish a principle upon which to base. We must know whether there is mind outside of man, or there is none, in order to decide whether mechanical or intellectual causes were active at the origin of species. It suffices to our present purpose to know, that the theories and hypotheses of homo-brutalism do not and can not refute our starting point in this inquiry, viz.: there is mind, and this will lead us on to the very objective point we seek to reach, the Cosmic God.

LECTURE IX.

ELEMENTARY ONTOLOGY.

Ladies and Gentlemen:—Nothing is more familiar and appears more wonderful to us than the nocturnal sky with its millions of silent and scintillating worlds floating mysteriously in the fathomless deep of the universe. Yet there is something more wonderful even than the stars, and that is the immense space in which they are mere sparks, like stations far apart, to serve as resting points to the mind, gazing on, and coursing through the vast and boundless expansion. It is extremely difficult to form a correct idea of space, if we begin to think that the mean distance of the Centauri from the earth is calculated at twenty billions of miles; that the distance of the Sirius is six time that of the Centauri, so that it takes its rays of light fifteen and one half years to reach our earth; and rising thus from constellation to constellation, according to magnitude, up to the milky-way, and the nebulae, and imagine that the rays of some stars take thousands of years to reach our earth, space appears too immense for the human mind; and yet we can hardly imagine how small a fraction of the universe that portion is which we, with our best telescopes, can discover from our standpoint on this earth. The most wonderful of all, however, by far more marvelous than stars and space, is man's mind with its self-consciousness, which knows both stars and space, and contemplates both to ascertain their mysteries not revealed to the eye. Man is nature's most profound mystery.

Before we can go on with our lectures, we must form some fundamental idea of the nature of this universe, in which and of which all things are. We must attempt to investigate and explain the nature, essential properties, and relations of all things as man comprehends them; and this science is called Ontology, from *onta*, "all things," and *logos*, "a discourse or exposition."

The first question in ontology is necessarily elementary. What is the primary element of which all these things are made? This, however, is the diverging point of the two systems of philosophy, known as materialism and spiritualism. In materialism, matter is the substance, and the forces inherent in matter create, preserve and govern all which is in this universe, mechanically and automatically. In spiritualism, spirit or mind is the substance, and the forces which create, preserve and govern all things in this universe, are manifestations of the will of that spirit, mind or intelligence.

We must first consider the claims of materialism as a philosophy, *i. e.*, a system of thoughts which expounds the universe with all its beings and their relations, as far as human reason and experience reach.

All materialists agree that there is only one substance in this universe, which is matter; still materialistic ontology is of two kinds, atomistic and dynamistic. Dynamistic ontology maintains, the primary element of the universe is force, and crossing forces produce and shape matter. Atomistic ontology maintains the primary element of the universe is matter, and this is the theory which we propose to investigate in this lecture.

Atomistic materialism starts out with the axiom, only that which the senses can perceive, capable of being sensually experienced, has existence in reality. All objects must appear bodily, moveable in space, and timely, changing with and in time. Matter filling space is the eternal and imperishable substratum of all being, motion and change. It consists primarily of its smallest parts, called atoms. The variety of the sensual objects depend on the different composition and configuration of the atoms by forces which exist in them and inseparable from them. All motion and generation in nature must be derived from the quantitive proportion of the atoms and their inherent forces of pressure and concussion. These two forces produce the entire mechanism of nature, and appear by the various configurations of the atoms as cohesion or organic life, as gravitation or Mr. Huxley's philosophizing brain, as the underlying and motor power of all that is, was, or will be, in molecule, planet, solar system or systems; the lion's roaring and preying, Cæsar crossing the Rubicon, the great American rebellion, and the Germans besieging Paris, prairie fires, burning forests, and the conflagration of Chicago, all facts, phenomena, thoughts, feelings, instincts, passions, deeds, and omissions, all which history and nature may show in all eternity, is the product of the atoms and their inherent forces of pressure and concussion. It is all one piece of mechanism, dead, and dumb, all inevitable necessity and blind casualty This I believe, is a fair and impartial statement of atomistic materialism as ontology, and we will for the sake of brevity call it atomism.

This atomistic ontology of an automatic universe, is usually illustrated by the ficticious spirit which La Place advanced. He supposes an omniscient spirit, one who knows all atoms and their inherent forces, together with all possible combinations which they are capable of entering in a sun or a crystal, a man's brain, or an infusorium. That spirit would also know all phenomena of nature, physical, moral and mental, which must occur in all eternity. As we calculate an eclipse or a transition in advance, that spirit could say, when, where, and why one will commit suicide, fall in love, establish an empire, or feel despondent on account of boots being too narrow, or a dinner spoiled; because all and every thing comes from the atom with its inherent forces of pressure and concussion.

According to atomism, you will readily understand æsthetics and ethics, freedom and virtue, individuality and character, merits and demerits, religion and morals, justice and duty, self-government and self-improvement, in brief, all that makes man and society, falls dead to the ground as an unwarranted superstition, unworthy of any enlightened naturalist ; as all and every thing depends upon the casual or necessary configuration of atoms and the resultants of diagonal and inherent forces, beyond the control of God or man, intelligence or fate, will or passion, beyond the control of nature itself. But this is no argument against atomism as a fact, for the materialist can say, the universe will not conform to your notions of utility or your desires of happiness. It is as it is, and where your notions and desires run contrary to the fact, you labor under error and self-delusion, which you had better correct as fast as you can. The spiritualist might reply to this, man and society being within the realm of nature, and according to materialism in perpetual revolt against her laws, then either man is supernatural, preternatual or any way above the laws of nature in certain respects ; or these laws of human nature, such as self-consciousness, freedom, duty, justice, virtue, are also natural laws; in either case atomism contains a fundamental error, as in the first case the atom and its forces govern not all things, and materialism is no philosophy, leaving phenomena unexplained and unknowable ; and in the second case the laws of nature are not that which atomism presents them to be, as the only focus in which they reveal themselves, in man's understanding, they produce freedom and rational intention and design, hence they are neither absolute necessity nor casualty. But we will not press this argument here, simply on account of its psychological nature it extends outside the scientific material under consideration.

The fundamental error of all materialism is in the self-delusion of attaching more certainty to matter outside of man than to his intelligence within himself. The things and the phenomena do not enter the mind in reality; we merely perceive them, we possess their images in our knowledge. The entire material world exists for us human beings as images of our imagination and ideas of our intelligence. Schopenhauer calls the consciousness of this truth the philosophical considerateness. Kant has made it the corner-stone of all philosophy, and no thinking man can deny it. All our knowledge is subjective, and in the first instance anthropomorphic. We carry over our thoughts, feelings and form into the objects of our observations. I see the muscles in a neighbor's face contract in a manner which I think to exhibit pain, or the contracting muscles move the lips to a smile, which I think exhibits pleasure. In both cases I only think so, because I have experienced pleasure and pain and a similar contraction of the muscles. I see tears issuing from a person's eye, and judge by the surrounding circumstances that these are the tears of joy or sorrow, because under similar circumstances I have also wept. The same is the case with all motions, gestures, and performances of man; we understand them only by interpretation of our own experience and feeling which we carry over to other men, because we think they are like us.

We do the same things precisely with the animals, and none has done it more extensively than Mr. Darwin. Except by interpretation of our own nature we know nothing of animal or vegetable psyche. We carry over our own thoughts, feelings and affects into the animal or even the vegetable, and adorn it with part of our own qualities and attributes and make it human in part, and then persuade ourselves to believe they are in the animal or vegetable, with how much truth, we shall discourse in another lecture.

Next we carry over our subjective thoughts, feelings, and affects into inanimate nature, and all become human organism, consisting of atoms, which are no more and no less than miniature men of materialistic imagination. Then we find in inorganic nature, life and functions, such as motion, sound, light and color. But there is no motion except in the intelligence which notes the change of place; in the universe as a whole everything is stationary. There is no sound in nature except for the ear of organic beings; it is all mere undulation of the air. There is no heat except for living creatures, no light and no color except for eyes similar to ours. All these impressions exist in our self-consciousness, and what is left of this universe of mechanical material construction is a mere automaton. The mechanism is here as completely as atomistic pressure and concussion can make it; but it is all dead, cold, dark, without thought and without feeling, none, not even the fictitious spirit of La Place can understand anything about it, because it has no attributes, no qualities, no manifestations, it is one solid piece of infinite machinery.

Therefore, the universe, in order to be knowable in the whole, or its parts, must first be enlivened, so to say, by intelligence after it has become an ideal reality in man's self-consciousness. Then intelligence and self-consciousness is the main power upon which we rely for any and every knowledge of the outer world. This must be most certain or we know nothing. But the atomist turns the whole upside-down, and starts out with the supposed axiom that the existence of the atoms and their inherent forces is more certain than my knowledge of myself. Here is the fundamental and radical error of all materialism as a philosophy. Philosophy must expound intelligence and self-consciousness and the relation of all objects thereto. All ontology begins with human nature. Therefore we opened this course of lectures with investigations into the human mind. For as long as we were not sure of mind, we could not possibly be sure of anything, since the things exist for us only as far as we are cognizant of them. But the atomist perverts the order of things. He is in the same condition with the man who maintains he has no eyes, nevertheless he is positive of the exactness and truthfulness of the objects of his vision.

Atomism maintains to possess positive knowledge of the nature of matter and its inherent forces, and adds self-satisfied, this is the only positive knowledge we do possess; although it has no means whatever to account for life, thought, sensation, feeling, consciousness, and kindred phenomena. Let us see how much truth is in the allegation. It is extremely easy and simple to maintain, that matter consists of the atoms, for it is a mere dissolution of a body into its smallest imaginable or thinkable parts, entirely empiric and arbitrary. But what is the nature of those atoms? The materialist can not tell any more or better the qualities of the atom than of a large body composed of them, or, *vice versa*; hence the theory explains nothing. An atom can not be imagined; for however small a particle of matter you imagine, it is always divisible, hence no atom which must be indivisible. If I dissolve the meteor, by destroying its inherent cohesion, I have primary matter. I dissolve this matter into its elements, by setting force against force, and the particles have become very small. I divide them ideally, and I have molecules. I reduce the molecule ideally to a point without dimensions, and I have no longer a material atom; I have a thought-thing, without material reality, something like the mathematical point, a purely metaphysical creature which is something and nothing at the same time. The material world, according to the atomists, consists of such atoms which are something and nothing. But a thing cannot be something and nothing at the same time. There is a contradiction in the terms. The atom can not be a material something, or else it must have dimensions, and be no longer an atom. Hence the atom is nothing. Many times nothing is always nothing; hence all matter consists of nothing. Here is the foundation of all atomistic philosophy. You see the atom is as rude a metaphysical creature, except as a scaffolding for chemistry and physics, as the hob-goblin of the African savage. In one case it is a ghost, and in the other a thing without dimensions, still material existence is claimed for both. Atomism first destroys the reality of matter and then maintains the existence of matter only is known with certainty. This is no philosophy, it is self-delusion.

But if we admit, the atomist's knowledge of matter is certain, we know next to nothing of the universe, by his method, and atomism is still no philosophy. This universe, or as much as we know of it, contains a small fraction of ponderable matter in proportion to its space. If you calculate the space which the solar system occupies and the bulk of matter in its various bodies according to their different degrees of density, you will find that matter composed of atoms is a small fraction in space. The constancy and universality of natural laws entitle to the conclusion that the same proportion of matter to space is universal. Matter occupies a small fraction in the immensity of space. Therefore, if we admit all and everything ever advanced by the atomists, we still know next to nothing of the universe. The atoms and their inherent forces can be thought in connection with ponderable matter only. This has existence in the worlds and their atmosphere only, and outside thereof is the universe in which those bodies float like points, without offering the least analogy of the two forms of existence; so that one of the ancient philosophers 'maintained, space is God. All atomistic theories taken as granted, they do not begin to expound the universe; hence atomism is no philosophy; and it is of no possible good to science except as a scaffolding to chemistry and physics, the latter even can do very well without it.

We can not be satisfied with atomism in our elementary ontology; because:

1. It maintains that we know with more certainty the existence and qualities of matter than the existence and revelations of our own mind in our self-consciousness.

2. It can not account for the existence of life, thought, sensation, feeling, self-consciousness, human nature, society, and history.

3. The fundamental idea of the atom is an absurdity, an incomprehensible and transcendental creature of empiricism, which negates the existence of matter.

4. The matter which might be said to consist of atoms is a small fraction of the space which offers no analogy to ponderable matter, so that one can not possibly explain the other.

Unable to explain the nature of things, their relations and connections, atomism is no philosophy, and we seek an ontology upon which to erect a philosophical system.

The question may justly be asked, if atomism is so absurd, how did it come to be defended by so many scientists? We will answer this question in our next lecture. Here we will only say that in Germany and France monism has succeeded atomism with many very respectable specialists. It is given up as an untenable position. Permit me also to add, that most scientists are rather poor philosophers. They hold to their school theories, in the main, as long as they possibly can. I have seen very, fine scientists who were one-sided and thoughtless sectarians in religion; and insignificant specialists and amateurs who were positive atheists, simply because neither of them ever went into an analysis of his thoughts. They can not philosophize.

LECTURE X.

HISTORY OF MATERIALISM.

Ladies and Gentlemen.—Before entering upon the main subject of this lecture, permit me to state that nothing can appear actualized in the monuments of mind, which is not in the mind. The energy must be there first before it can be realized. Whatever is not in man he can not do. Therefore we look upon all monuments of actualized mind in the works and history of man as equally necessary in the great drama of history. The superstitions of the savage, in the process of man's developments, are as necessary as the religion, philosophy, and science of cultural nations. If it were not necessary, it would not be.

I make this statement in order not to be misunderstood in regard to either science or religion. Both of them are, for the consideration of philosophy, mental elements. Their connection appears to me in history thus:

The human mind, when it first began to think consciously, capable of abstraction and reflection, was idealistic. The mind set itself outside of itself in ideals of religion and art. Both are the offspring of spontaneous inspiration, and creative of axiomatic truth, with the desire to realize them in man and society, or in works of art. Both are boundless. They break through the limits of reality, or even probability, into the infinite, and are liable to roam upon the broad ocean of phantasy, far beyond the secure haven of sober truth.

Error always produces practical results painful to man and society, irritates the reasoning faculty, and challenges resistance. This gives rise to philosophy, which stops the erratic reveries; and calls the products of the mind before the judgment seat of reason, to establish an equilibrium between the work of spontaneity and the force of reality, to arrive at approximate truth.

Again, philosophy is after all speculative, consequently liable to the influence of phantasy. Like religion and art, it is engaged in the solution of problems pointing to the infinite, so that it often leaves the *terra firma* of reality. Nevertheless it can not desert this ground entirely, therefore expounds, shapes, and forms it, to harmonize with the main idea or theory of the peculiar system. This leads to grave errors as well as to great discoveries in natural science. Here come in again the errors, the painful results, the irritation and challenge of reason; which rouses the mind to another species of activity, the investigation of special provinces of reality, research, and experiment, to establish facts and laws of the things as they are in essence and function. So science corrects philosophy, as philosophy corrects religion and art.

On the other hand, however, it must be admitted that religion and art produce the material for philosophy, and philosophy produces the ideas for science, which returns its results to philosophy. Again, philosophy in regard to religion and art must be skeptical and critical, must doubt, analyze, reject and adopt, in order to construct; and science must be skeptical and critical in relation to philosophy in the same manner and for the same reason. Still it is only from the harmony of these three elements of our knowledge, and these three methods of our cognition, that truth rises in her sublime beauty and majestic grandeur.

Besides the numerous benefits of practical life and the progress of intelligence resulting from natural science, it acts also as the centripetal force on philosophy, religion, and art, which are centrifugal in their very nature. It calls them back to the facts of material reality. Therefore no rational man will expect of the scientist that, in his science, he be anything but a materialist. Nature must explain itself. He has no use for miracles or any divine interposition, as long as he seeks the facts and laws of matter. Nor can it be expected of the scientist to adopt the method of cognition, peculiar to religion, art, or philosophy. He must have his own, because his field of labor is peculiar to itself. All that is expected of him is not to arrogate to himself all knowledge of all truth, to the exclusion and negation of all other provinces of mental activity.

Therefore, whatever I might say about materialism as a philosophy, can not and does not refer to the method of the natural sciences, which I think is perfectly correct, or personally to any scientist, who must do his work in his own way in order to do it well. I have nothing to say against specialists, as most all scientists proper are. I merely review the philosophical attempts of speculative scientists—some of them do not even deserve this title—to deify matter and establish new creeds of scientific dogmas, as men like Vogt, Moleschot, Buechner, Haeckel, Huxley, and Tyndal do. I investigate to discover the worth of their pretensions. Now let us go to history.

When in ancient Greece mythology had run through its natural cycle, the classical poets had poured forth their best of the beautiful and the true, and the sculptors had carved out the ideas of cold marble, error challenged reason, which took hold upon the accumulated material, and opened the history of formal philosophy. with Thales, Hippo, Aneximenes, Anaximander, and Heraclit. The starting point was one upon which the theology of that day had heaped myth, and explained nothing. It was the problem of the stability of being and the mobility of beings. Nothing remains as it is and what it is, yet all remains the same forever. The mind attempted to penetrate the realms of mutations in search of the immutable cause.

It must not be expected of those thinkers that they solved the problem, although they prepared it well for future reasoners. They were not acquainted with the principles of mind and intelligence. They had no psychology, no formal logic, and no idea of universal intelligence; hence the question reduced itself to the nature of matter, in which the solution of the problem was sought. Without knowledge of natural laws, or even forces, their speculations on matter were crude, and in many instances childish. Without science they could hardly be otherwise. The results of a long cycle of speculation, with the exception of two abstract ideas, causation and being, were very meagre, and like the starting point and paganism the world over, materialistic, first in the form monism, which considers all the universe one consecutive mass of matter with the cause of motion within itself, and motion as the cause of all other phenomena in nature. Matter continually brings forth individual beings, and absorbs them again as the waves rise from the ocean to fall back again. Then followed the rude analysis of matter into three and finally four elements with the problem, which of the elements predominates in universal causation? At last philosophical analysis went beyond the elements, imagined matter to consist originally of the smallest thinkable parts, called atoms, in which the cause of all motion and being is permanent forever.

Strabo thinks the Phœnician Moshus was the author of the atomistic hypothesis. Laertius and Cicero were of the opinion that Leukipp invented it, Anyhow it was introduced in Grecian philosophy by Democritus, the well-known laughing philosopher, sometime between 470 and 460 B. C., with whom everything, also the gods, was an aggregate of atoms. On the other hand, Pythagoras (540 to 510 B. C.) and the Italian school, had introduced the mysticism of numbers, and expounded the universe by the mysteries of mathematics.

Extensive travels in the East, especially in Egypt, Phœnicia, and Syria, then the centers of culture, and the close intercourse with the then dominant Persians, gradually brought other ideas into Greece, so that in the fourth century B. C., Socrates, Plato, Aristotle, and their disciples, made an end to the more ancient materialism, and built up those systems of philosophy, including the natural sciences, which have exercised so vast an influence upon the progress of man, and still do in very many instances, so that besides the Bible, Plato and Aristotle were the main factors of civilization. Still materialism had two more prominent disciples, Epicurus and Lucretius, who took up and expounded the atomic hypothesis: but they were read and studied only after the cycle of classical philosophy had been closed, and moral corruption had taken a firm hold of the Roman, whom the Stoics with their stern ethics could not satisfy.

It must be borne in mind that materialism was not the fruit of science: it was metaphysical, set into the world in ages of myths, crude speculation, and considerable ignorance; it was the first attempt at philosophy.

The conquests and subsequent corruption of Rome, the advent of Christianity, and the construction of a huge despotism, made an end to philosophy, until the Arabs, a century after Mohammed, took up again the Grecian literature, and with it also the classical philosophy. Arabs and Jews, with the exception of a few Christian scholasts, were the expounders of philosophy in the Middle Ages down to the revival of letters in England. Also among those Arabs and Jews, a materialistic school sprang up under the name of *Kelam*, which continued the atomistic theories, with the only addition of a Supreme Being, who was to them the Creator and governor of the atoms; and one of those philosophers was the celebrated Ibn Gabriol. Saadia already, and after him a number of Jewish reasoners down to Moses Maimonides, discussed atomistic theory, and advanced nearly all and the same arguments against it which are in vogue now; but our common historiographers are not aware of these facts.

In Christendom, however, there is no trace of atomism before Gassendi. This Pierre Gassendi, the learned Frenchman (1592 to 1655) philosopher and mathematician, the friend of Keppler and Galileo, cotemporary and opponent of Descartes, reproduced and enlarged the system of Epicurus and Lucretius. At the same time Thomas Hobbes (1588 to 1679) advanced his materialistic system in England, and found numerous admirers and disciples. These two men started materialism in Christendom, and gave the impulse to the revival of natural science.

Polemical discussions over materialism, in France, Germany, England and Holland, were almost continual in the last part of the 17th and the 18th centuries. In France which had no philosopher between Diderot and Comte, and hardly any religion, materialism produced atheism, which reached its highest point in the age of reason. In Germany, the philosophers, and especially Immanuel Kant overcame atheistic materialism, but succumbed also after Kant to Spinoza's pantheism, which is not hostile to science. In England which had no philosophers after Locke and Hume, the religious feeling overcame materialism and turned it into the peculiar English deism Atomism was retained among scientists, more as a scaffolding of chemistry than a principle. Between the days of Robert Boyle (1626 to 1692), the founder of the royal society, and John Dalton (1766 to 1844) both chiefly chemists, the conceptions concerning atoms were frequently modified, especially through the influence of Isaac Newton's discoveries, as was the case also after Dalton had established his theory of matter. None ever thought of constructing a philosophical system on the atomistic basis. Scientists were mostly Spinozists, panthesists or deists of some kind. This gave England and France the advantage, that their scientists speculated less and worked more successfully for the advancement of industry and commerce, while Germany was still engulfed in transcendental speculation. The modern English philosophers of nature have been dragged from the practical field by German influence, as we shall see instantly, and cling to atomism merely from scholastic prejudice. The main naturalists who established atomism.

in science were Englishmen of great influence. It is now the system of the schools, over which Mr. Tyndal could not come without considerable trouble.

What Cromwell and his Ironsides have done for England and the revolution for France, philosophy and science are doing slowly for Germany and Austria. Up to the year 1830 Germany poetized, philosophized, was dogishly loyal and transcendentally patriotic. The wretched results of 1830 sent the patriots to prisons or into exile; priests, professors, and artists were impressed into the service of absolutism, in State and church. Metternich's policy governed Austria, Germany, Italy, and partly also France. Jesuits and priests were his tools and he was their patron.

The period of philosophy and poetry closed and there was a painful vacuum in the German mind, to observe, that there was in the neighboring countries of Western Europe not only more liberty and more popular power, but also more wealth and prosperity. It was discovered that the church, both Catholic and Protestant, was the right hand power of the despotism, under which all persons and things groaned; and that philosophy had been turned into a transcendental quibbling, to support church dogmas and retard the progress of science.

The wrath of the sufficiently cultivated German scholars, liberals and patriots, was turned first against the weakest of the two great powers, against the church. All works of fiction, in order to be popular, had to be anti-Christian.

Feuerbach, Schopenhaur and Czolbe did, from the philosophical standpoint, the same work as Strauss with his Life of Jesus, Bruno Bauer, the New Catholics, the Free Congregations and their head leaders from the critical and practical standpoints. Dogmatic Christianity was undermined among the middle classes, which were pleased with the scorning frivolity of Heinrich Heine and his confreres, and a peculiar atheism sprung up, unreasoning and fanatical, which had no justification in its own behalf except the hatred felt against Church and State.

Meanwhile the scientists of Germany emancipated themselves from both theology and philosophy, and achieved great victories upon all scientific fields, so that science had become the only field of activity for the German mind. Science was popular, profitable and independent. So the ground was prepared for Vogt, Moleschott, Buechner, Haeckel, and other apostles of mechanical ontology, to do away not only with church and priest, but also with the cause of both, God, soul, religion, freedom, and traditions; to do away with all philosophy forever, and commence history anew on the two new dogmas of the new creed:

1. This world with all that is therein is a piece of a blind mechanism without intelligence or final cause, the work of necessity and casualty.

2. There is only one way to arrive at truth, observation and experiment, whatever cannot be conceived by the senses, exists not.

So the school of modern materialism opened in Germany, Its influence on England is evident, especially in Darwin's Descent of Man to which Haeckel lately added his Anthropogenie, to place man into the back ground of all animals. The blunders and arrogance of Church and State in Germany and Austria, not science, are the causes of modern materialism, and a thorough reformation of both, radical in its character, will be the end thereof in this cycle of history. The nineteenth century can not go back to the old Paganism and the crude philosophy of Democrit and Epicure. Such a retrogression is impossible. We can not maintain society now on the materialistic creed. Neither the statesman and jurist nor the philosopher derives any benefit from it, and the community will not part with the ideals which make life tolerable, virtue sacred, and freedom man's natural birthright. We can not do without human nature as long as we are men; but materialism as it is now negates all human dignity and aspirations. The fanaticism against Church and State is a retribution, a necessary evil, a painful sore of the impure blood, which heals already, since the unification of Germany and the liberalization of Austria. Materialism is a necessary evil, as long as the church undergoes not a radical change; but it is no philosophy, which explains the universe or affords a sound substratum for the construction of society. It will die out with the causes which re-produced it. It always comes with corruption in public institutions, and disappears at the approach of adequate reformation.

Ridiculous, supremely so, indeed, appears to us the crude materialism of some of our American writers, who repeat slavishly what Germans and Englishmen have said, in many cases years ago, and often refuted since then. They adopt a poisonous medicine without evil in the social organism to be remedied. Our State affairs are independent of the church, and our priests and preachers are harmless creatures, and without influence on public affairs. Some of our materialists are mere amateurs in science and children in philosophy. Others have heard or read so long ago, and are too indolent to hear, read, or think again. I can pay no regard to them in these lectures, and expect, they will neither hear nor read them. I am ready now to continue my regular course, and will continue in my next lecture on elementary ontology.

LECTURE XI.

DYNAMIC ONTOLOGY.

LADIES AND GENTLEMEN.—The question we discuss is, Is matter or force the substance of the beings in this universe? If matter is, then the ontology is materialistic; if force is, then it is dynamistic, as the Greek dynamis signifies power or force. Let us see what we know about matter.

The atoms of speculative science are metaphysical points without reality; therefore they cannot be accepted either as the substratum of matter or the starting point of ontology.

With the atoms of speculative science the atomic forces also fall to the ground; especially as the latter are no more than abstractions of observable forces, arbitrarily attributed to imaginary atoms, so that we know no more and no better of atomic forces than of those observable in the bulk of compound matter.

The atoms of chemistry have extension and weight; hence they bear no analogy whatever to the atoms of speculative science.

There are as many kinds of atoms as there are elements, viz., sixty-three, inclusive of Professor Bunsen's coesium and robedium, thirteen non-metalic and fifty metalic; so that we know now of sixty-three kinds of matter.

The molecule, which is an aggregate of atoms, is the smallest bulk of matter perceptible, and is supposed to possess all the attributes observable in the large bulk.

The molecule may be an aggregate of atoms of two or more kinds of matter; and there are as many kinds of molecules as there are chemical compounds.

Matter is inert, passive, and imperceptible, except by its qualities; it is moved, made active and perceptible by the forces which work on or in it, so that each quality of matter is a manifestation of force.

When we say we see matter, we mean to say that we

see something which reflects light; hence we see the manifestation of a force. When we say that we can touch matter, we mean to say that we can place our hands upon something which offers resistance; hence we have a sensation of that force. When Du Bois says the particle of iron is always the same thing, whether in the wheel of a railroad car, in a meteor, or in the blood, he means to say it is perceptible in the same manner, if effected by the same forces. The human mind can perceive ideas only, and these are expressed in matter by the changes to which the forces subject it.

Matter is the residuum of bulk, mass, or body, after all forces are separated, a residuum which can not be analyzed any further, because it is imperceptible. The physicist and mathematician have to do with the forces exclusively, paying no attention to matter. The chemist investigates and contemplates the various processes of composition and decomposition by the forces which act in or upon matter.

Matter itself is equally unknown to all of them, and is no factor in either science; because it is imperceptible. You take away the force of molecular cohesion or attraction and you reduce the solid, granite or meteor, to a fluid, then to gas, then to ether, *i. e.*, to zero, imperceptible to man, because it has no qualities, no forces exercise a perceptible influence on it. Let the forces play again on the ficticious zero of matter, and it changes again into ether, gas, fluid, and solid, again perceptibe to man; *i. e.*, you can not perceive the zero, but you perceive the forces operating on it and manifesting themselves through it.— This will mislead none to deny the existence of matter, for it always remains the substratum of perceptible beings, although matter without force is unknowable, and it may well be the creature of crossing forces.

On the other hand, we are too well used to bulk, body, and mass, to think of matter without force being imperceptible; and yet it cannot be denied that some time ago this very bulk, body, and mass, free of certain force, was imperceptible, can be made so again by the chemist, and is made so continually by the earth's evaporation and metamorphosis of particles akin to exhalation, which forms the atmosphere.

The very coal which heats your rooms, engenders steam in your engines, or the matter which now forms the bodies of your trees, was a little while ago imperceptible carbon, and your fires change it continually into the same state of imperceptibility. You see whether matter at the last instance is not the creature of crossing forces, without materiality, bulk, body, or mass, is a question not very easily decided.

It must be admitted, anyhow, that anything in this universe we can perceive, know, or think is rendered perceptible and knowable by dynamic or static forces. We know of this phenomenal world, the various manifestations of forces, and no more. We can not build science on what we know not. Being entitled to build upon that only which we do know, and we certainly know the forces by their manifestations, we can adhere to dynamistic ontology only ; and the only question from our standpoint can be, whether dynamicism and spiritualism are not identical.

The atomists understand this point well, and being unable to deny the existence of force, resort to the hypothesis that matter and force are in fact one and the same thing. There is no matter without force, and no force without matter. The two terms are attributes of the same substance, two abstractions of the same subject; or also matter possesses force, *i. e.*, matter is the subject, and force the predicate ; matter is, and force is its function. This explains not attractions at great distances, the theory of light, or the parallelogram of forces; but the atomist says he advances the best hypothesis at his command.

Here the difficulties of atomism are numerous. The theory, on which those very same materialists rely, leads irresistably to the negation of matter, consequently also to the negation of force, so that nothing remains. The nothingness of the atom multiplied infinitely with itself, has always for its product the nonentity of matter. If force is the function of matter, which is not, then force also exists not. If both matter and force are attributes of the same substance, and matter is not, then it follows that force alone is the conceivable attribute of the unknown substance, and dynamicism is established upon the ruins of atomism.

The only materialist of high authority known to me who makes a plain confession of this difficulty is Du Bois. He says this: "If one asks what remains, if neither force nor matter possesses reality, then those who stand with me upon the same standpoint will reply thus: "It is not given to the human mind in these things to reach beyond a last contradiction," etc. "We possess sufficient renunciation to submit to the idea that at last all science reaches the limit, not to comprehend the essence of things, but to show the impossibility of such comprehension. So in mathematics, it is not the quadrature of the circle, or in mechanics, the *perpetuum mobile*, which science must discover; it must show the impossibility thereof." Helmholz makes similar confessions.

However, this declaration of insufficiency merely says, from the atomistic standpoint, we reach in its last result in reality the nothing and in formality the contradiction; to which I take the liberty to add, therefore the atomistic standpoint is erroneous. You misunderstand the nature of matter, then you make force to a function of misunderstood matter, to land finally in contradiction and absurdity. The results of science are correct, because they are not influenced by your theory. Invert the proposition, say force is the subject and matter the predicate, force is active and matter passive, force is perceptible and matter is not, force exists independent of matter, although manifested therein only to human senses; and science certainly losses nothing, for science must establish laws which are in force only, and all those last contradictions fall dead to the ground. That such is the fact without personification or poetical dreams is certainly demonstrable.

Matter can be freed of some forces acting upon it, and others can be conducted into it, as is done every day; hence force and matter are separable and not identical, not in the abstract but in reality. You stamp or grind a solid body to particles, are you not expelling the force which connected them to a compact mass? You dissolve a powdered material to a fluid, are you not expelling force again? You transform the fluid into gas, have you not again expelled force by force? You weigh the solid, then the powder, the fluid and the gas, have you not precisely the same weight in all instances? Here is evidently force expelled without loss of matter; therefore force must be immaterial and separable from matter. It is not a mere function of matter, and not being function, it must be substance. If you perform the chemical process, downward from gas to a lump of coal, you arrive at the same results precisely by conducting force into matter, and you are entitled to the same conclusions.

Take another view of the matter. Take for instance Gay-Lussac's discovery, made in 1808, that different gases under equal pressure and temperature, are united to one body according to the simple volume proportion, so that the volume of the compound stands in simple proportion to the volume of its ingredients. Here you make one body of two or more, not by molecular force, without any change of weight. Two forces, pressure and heat, have been conducted into the matter, and changed its condition, yet these forces were evidently not in that matter which you changed, and being in now, show neither extension nor weight. They must be immaterial and independent of matter.

Again, we can see the independence of force from matter as often as we look heavenward. Where the atmosphere of our earth ceases, there is the end of matter—there begins space. The same is the case if looked on from every other mundane body. Space beyond the atmosphere is not filled with matter. The ancient atomists were consistent enough to adopt the vacuum; with them space is a vacuum. If all motion is in the atoms, then each must be in a vacuum in which to move; so must be every body composed of atoms. The moving body must have vacant space. The moving body cannot occupy the same space occupied by other bodies. Our knowledge of mechanics makes the case still worse. If the earth, or any other body, would meet with perpetual resistance, its motion must be perpetually retarded, and it must come to a final suspension of motion, not in billions of years, as the usual calculation runs, but in a very few myriads of years.

If so, the retardation of planetary motion must have become observable somewhere; which, however, is not the case. All theories basing upon space resistance are illegitimate, because they rest upon not a single established fact. On the contrary, all facts known of planetary motion, demonstrate that there is no resistance in space, and no friction.

In modern times, some atomists advance the hypothesis that every atom moves in a sphere of force, which is already a confession that force is immaterial and independent. But then comes the chief difficulty. Our earth receives light and heat from the sun, and moves by the force of attraction exercised by the central luminary. The sun exercises the same influence on all planetary bodies as far distant as to Neptune—2,853,600,000 miles; and probably beyond this. Furthermore, we suppose to know that a mutual attraction of the planets for each other exists, as we do know that every planet receives light from every other planet. Hence the whole space of the solar system is continually penetrated by the forces of light, heat, and attraction in lines crossing each other in all imaginary angles. If all fixed stars are suns and centers of solar systems, then all space is continually under the same influences. If our solar system is not an independent section of the universe, then either all suns must exercise mutual attraction, or move around a central sun; in either case all space is filled with these forces crossing each other in all possible angles.

Here is the great difficulty of atomism. Forces being evidently at work in the immense space, it is no vacuum. If force is a function of matter, all space must be filled with matter, call it ether or zero. All matter consisting of atoms, space is an infinite continuation of atoms. But there rise a number of questions, first in regard to motion; how can the earth or any other body pass through the space filled with atoms? If we say the solid body by its superior resistance and velocity dislodges the atoms from the space it passes, to which they always return after it is vacated; then the space atoms must be highly elastic, capable of being compressed, and communicating the pressure from atom to atom. Where is that pressure to stop, and what can stop it? Each atom in this case being agitated by two forces, its own and the impulse given it by the moving body, and each atom behind it by only one force. Where is the resistance in space to stop that motion of motion? If stopping somewhere anyhow by means unknown, then the pressure and temperature of the moving body, according to Gay-Lussac's experiment, acting on the atoms must unite them, and united they must be attracted by the earth; then the body of the earth must grow continually, which we know to be not the case.

Again a body is elastic, if its particles can be compressed, i. e. they can change place and occupy the space of their pores. Hence elastic atoms must be such whose parts can change place. Therefore every space atom must consist of parts and be no atom. You may divide each atom as much as you please; you have the same question at the smallest thinkable atom; you arrive precisely at the same absurdity. Therefore there can be no space atoms; but there is force in space, hence force is independent and immaterial.

Next comes the question of conductors of force in the space. On what pinions do these forces travel? If we imagine light, heat and attraction issuing from the sun as forces, the corpuscular theory having become impossible, they must strike every atom around that luminary, then every atom so moved communicates this motion to the adjoining layer of atoms, and so on, as the ring of waves enlarge, down through the entire solar system to Neptune, until this motion is received and reflected or revibrated by the various solid bodies. If so, every atom in the solar system outside the bodies must be perpetually and incessantly engaged in receiving and communicating these motions, as those forces work on without the slightest intermission and work upon every point in the space. In this case, it might be intelligible, how light, heat, and attraction reach the earth from the sun; but there is not the slightest room left for the light and attraction which the planetary bodies send to each other. All space atoms being continually engaged by the energy passing from the sun, no medium whatever is left, to conduct force from planet to planet, much less from solar system to solar system, and nobody can tell how we can see the stars or recognize the attractive influence of the planets. But we do see the stars, light, heat and attraction work alike all over the universe, hence the theory of space atoms falls dead to the ground.

Next in order comes the theory of Mr. Rankin, in which I can see a mere subterfuge, although very poetical. The atoms are not supposed to be displaced, but revolve around their cylindrical axes, as the waves of light or other forces pass them.

This does not remove the difficulties just discussed, and brings in also the question of elasticity. There must evidently be vacant space between those revolving atoms, or else they could not revolve; or, as the sun force strikes them, they must be compressed to pass the force. The first case is impossible, because there can be no vacuum, and the second is impossible on account of the nature of elasticity. Besides, what is that sun force which passes the revolving atoms? If it also consists of atoms, then atom dislodges atom continually in all space, it is all wheel within wheel in perpetual motion; and the first question recurs; for there is evidently no room left for any other force function in all space. If it is dynamic force which rolls over the revolving atoms, well then, there is force independent and immaterial, and we have no use for revolving atoms, or any other space-atoms, as independent and immaterial force is its own conductor.

Atomism, from whatever standpoint you examine it, is impossible. But it is certain that, whatever we know or can know of this physical world, whatever science knows or can know thereof, is the manifestation of force. Therefore we must stop at dynamic ontology, and say, we know of this physical world that which manifesting forces reveal to our senses and cognition. This must be the basis of all science and of all philosophy. Force is immaterial and independent. It is omnipresent and almighty, in this physical world. It is bound to no time, and no space where there is no material obstacle, and governs all material things. The laws of nature are the laws of force working upon matter.

Here is the grave of all materialism as a philosophy; and here begins philosophy proper. Force immaterial and independent of matter, the existence of which no rational observer can justly doubt, although it is neither bulk, body, or mass, and perceptible in its manifestations only, is the central point of all philosophy. It is Spinoza's substance, Kant's intelligible world, Hegle's absolute idea; Schopenhauer's will, and Hartman's Unbewusstes. Each of them has viewed this central thought from another standpoint. There is truth and error in each and all of them. Let us see what we can adopt and what we must correct. We have now gained two important points, mind and force. Let us now investigate whether there is mind in force, or in other words, whether this omnipresent and almighty force is intelligent, whether it is physical, psychical, unconscious or conscious, whether it is mechanical or has a will, or to be short, whether it is infinite madness or infinite Deity. This will be the subject of my next lectures.

LECTURE XII.

BIOLOGY.

What is life? This is a sorrowful question with many who either feel its heavy burden, or are doomed to testify to its uncertainty, when friends are laid low, and leave a painful vacuum in the aching heart. But this is not the question I feel to-day able to discuss. I do not wish to impose tears on you. What is life, is also in science a very important question. It is a special science called Biology, from the Greek *bios* "life," and *logos* "discourse" or "treatise," the science which treats of the force or forces of life in general, as manifested in the vegetable and animal kingdoms. Any conception of ontology without a settled principle of biology is necessarily imperfect; especially as this earth appears to be the mere pedestal upon which the living beings rest or move; forces and elements apparently have but one aim, viz.: to produce and sustain life.

My definition of life is this: Life is the differentiation of vital force which produces and develops individual organism and preserves its identity. I say this is my definition, for the definitions of English scientists and philosophers are bewildering and mostly illogical; because they are based upon mechanical atomism, which denies the existence of vital force. Buechner advanced the formula which most all of them repeat in different words. He says, "Thought, spirit, soul, are nothing material, not themselves body; they are the complex of homogenous forces grown together to a unity." He adds then, "At least we would not know, how to define spirit or force except as something immaterial, something which excludes matter and is its opposite." This is the oracle of the English scientists and also of Mr. Spencer. Life being a complex of homogenous forces grown together to a unity, of course, there is no vital force.

Philosophically, this is impossible, for things immaterial can not grow together and form a unity, as growing together means the connection of all points in two surfaces. Souls, spirits, thoughts cannot possible grow together. Physically, the theory is overthrown · by the constancy of each force in the parallelogram of forces. If life was a complex of forces, each of them must be traceable in the process. But life is not sound, heat, attraction, or electricity; none of which is discoverable in the principle which maintains the identity of the individual, notwithstanding all other natural forces working against it and effecting its dissolution as soon a life departs.

Evidently we have before us in every living organism a force which governs the others for this specific purpose. Every constant relation of elements or bodies to one another, points to an overruling force in action for this specific purpose. In the organic kingdoms, the immense variety of elementary relations to form and sustain here a tree, there a shrub, here an herb and there a blade of grass, here a mollusk, there a radiate or articulate, here a reptile, fish, bird, or mammal, and there a man, all made up of the same elements, governed by the same forces, necessitates us to adopt an overruling force which subjects matter and force, in order to assume this shape and no other. to be so large at its birth and grow so far and no farther, have this form, surface and color and no other, develop and live so long and no longer. All these limitations and modifications point to a special force at work which we call vital force.

This vital force bears no similiarity to the other natural forces, to electricity, light, heat, sound, or mechanical motion. The most wonderful effect produced by physical forces is in the crystal. Yet Du-Bois-Reymond who considers life "a very difficult mechanical problem," admits in the same passage, that crystal and organism differ from one another like the mere walls of a factory and the artistical machineries which give it name and character. The most brilliant diamond has no more in common with the lowest organism than a flake of snow with the hydraulic elevators in your stores or hotels. In the lowest organism is life, motion, assimulation and secretion, none of which is in the most beautiful crystal. The crystal forms of the minerals are mathematically fixed, so that in the detail, the relations of angles and planes to the crystalographic axis is unchanged. But the organic form can not be mathematically fixed. It is free in every individual. Starting from the round cell, its outlines assume the most wonderful variety. There is no necessity in the relation of angles and planes to the axis. Every plant and every animal develops its arch type with a certain degree of freedom and variability, which must be the effect of a cause not at work in the inorganic world, for which we have no better name than vital force.

The mechanical atomists, must banish life from the universe, in order to have a dead mechanism. But here it is in the organic kingdoms; how can it appear here, if it is not there? How can an effect be produced without a cause? They treat this question as that professor did his visitor whose queries he could not answer; he sat the man out doors, and all problems were solved. We have no dogma to defend and may treat the question with a little more courtesy.

Like the general survey, so the investigation into the particulars of this phenomenon will lead us to the existence of vital force. Helmholz is honest enough to stop short at the very sensible theory: "Either organic life has commenced sometime to exist, or it has existed from eternity." This is a plain admission of ignorance as to the origin of life.

On our planet, this is certain, life had a beginning.— The geologist has examined into the crust of this earth and traced life from its most simple start, both in number and form, in structure and size, to the Flora and Fauna of this day, with man at the head of 25,000 genera of vertebrates. The earth is supposed to consist of a central and perpetual fire encased in a molten metallic mass of primitive and unstratified rock, with a solid nucleus for its center. Around this mother rock the crust of the earth has been formed in successive ages of convulsions and revolutions. The crust next to the mother rock, called the Archean age, shows no remains of organic life. The next crust called the Silurian age contains organic rocks, in which the lowest forms of organic life, small in number and simple in construction, are imbedded. There are the algae representing the vegetable kingdom, some radiates, mollusks and articulates, representing the animal kingdom, which must have lived in water much more salted and thicker than our sea water. One step higher, there is the crust or stratum called the Devonian age, in which fishes and two higher types of marine vegetables make their appearance. Again one step higher, and we arrive at the Carboniferous age, in which reptiles have left their remains, and they increase upward to the next or Secondary age. Above this, we arrive at the stratum called the Terrtiary age, and there for the first time we meet mammals, dicotyls and palms. There is the beginning of the large animals and trees of our earth's surface, upon which at last man appears, creation's last and most wonderful work. The law of progression is well recorded in the rocks, so that we can trace back the history of organic life to its unquestionable beginning on this globe, and read its progressions from stage to stage up to man and his surroundings.

The first and lowest animal or plant which made its appearance on this globe was made up of organic matter which, in its morphotic structure and inherent force is entirly different from inorganic matter. All organic beings, from the lowest sea weed to man, are composed of cells, some of which are so minute that they can be examined only under the most powerful magnifier. Still the smallest as the largest cell is a thing of its own in morphotic structure and inherent force. Of some of the cells, though by no means of all, we know the form, structure, chemical ingredients and their proportions; but the force which unites those ingredients in those proportions to an organic cell of that particular nature is a profound mystery.

These cells of which all animate beings are made, which form the starting point of every organism, and make up all its tissues and organs, bones, blood, muscles or nerves, root, stem, bark, or fruit, are little bags, as may be best observed in the cells of the common elder pith or the coarse cells of the orange. The envelop, called the cell-wall or membrance, contains a fluid or gelatinous matter and some round particles or granules, in which the center of the cell is formed. These cells are of different shapes and chemical composition, not only in different individuals, but also in the different parts of the same body. The long thread-like cells which give the fibrous character to the flesh, do not differ originally from the cells which build up the brain, blood and bone, glands, nerves, and arteries. So throughout the whole living organism, the cells constituting different tissues have their peculiarities for each, and yet originally all the cells are alike. Without any scientific investigation taste informs us, that the various vegetables and the parts of different animals whose flesh we eat, are composed of different cells, in regard to chemical constituents, and yet the microscope shows but one and the same kind of cells. Nature constructs the grape, the orange, the chicken, the pigeon, of cells, made for this very purpose; so the brain, blood, bone, muscle, lung, etc., are composed of cells fit only for this and no other purpose.

The construction of these tens of thousands of chemically different cells, made of the same elements, to make up the various kinds of vegetable and animal organism, and in each organism the different parts, and the parts of parts, fitted together by the *blastema* or *matrix* in the animal, is the fundamental mystery of organic life, for which none of the known forces of nature give us the least account. And yet these cells grow, fill up, divide, live, change perpetually their constituents in the organic body only, and are transformed into inorganic matter as soon as life is defunct. So we have before us unquestionably a series of phenomena most wonderful and intricate, entirely different in kind from all others known to science, and peculiar to themselves only; phenomena which point forcibly to a different agent, for which we have but one name, and this is vital force.

Please, ladies and gentlemen, not to forget the thread of my humble argument. Organic life is a phenomenon entirely different from all others. It is not the complex of the known forces of light, heat, sound, electricity, attraction or mechanical motion, much less of the atomic forces. Where then is the definition of life by our English cotemporaries, Mr. Spencer's included? Evidently nowhere. Life had a beginning on this globe, and all our knowledge testifies that it could appear in organic matter only, in the cell or cells. The cell either made itself, which no naturalist will admit, or there must be vital force. Therefore the atomists hard pressed with the pertinent question, how did the cell come into existence? resort to various dodges and subterfuges. The first is the *generatio equivoca*, which means the production of cells or organic beings from inorganic matter in an unknown manner. In my opinion the argument amounts to nothing. It pushes the question back a little way without changing it. The question would still be, by which force is inorganic matter transformed into organic, the inanimate into animate? and the answer would be again vital force. Mr. Schwan, the father of our knowledge of the cells, denies the possibility of *generatio equivoca*. In France a long and bitter controversy was carried on on this very subject, with Mr. Pasteur and the academy on one side,

Pouchet, Joly, and Mussett on the other, without any result contrary to Schwan's assertion. In Germany, it was Carl Vogt who maintained the *generatio equivoco*, but without any support from the numerous and shrewd experiments to this end, by prominent scientists. At last it was finally demonstrated in Pfluegner's laboratory, that water boiled a certain length of time was incapable of breeding infusoria, because the germs were destroyed by heat, showing conclusively the fallacy of *generatio equivoca*. The last of great scientists, in our country, Prof. Agassiz, has shown in one of his last lectures "All life from the egg;" hence this dodge is dead.

Next in order come the monads, the most simple of microscopic organism, mere points of living beings, now considered vegetable spores or germs. Mr. Haeckel refers to a little marine creature, described by Mr. Huxley and named *Bathybius Haeckelii*, mere little slime bags supposed to live in the ocean at a depth of 12,000 to 24,000 feet, as the beginning of organisms. The question is, whether those monads, Bathybii and the like creatures, are not organic remains of larger beings which died and dissolved in the salt water. It appears they are. But if they are not, it has no bearing on the main question.— Whether any morphotic structure by a monad, Bathybius, protoplasm, spore, germ, red snow, gory dew, elephant, or man, it is under all circumstances something different from inorganic matter; it lives and the question always is the same, by what force? On the contrary, those miniature beings without any discoverable organism go far to prove, that life is no mechanical problem; it depends on no mechanism; life is prior to the mechanism in which it manifests itself.

Therefore Mr. Haeckel himself is not satisfied with his Bathybian proof, and advances this: "If you do not adopt the hypothesis of *generatio eguivoca* (Urzeugung), then at this simple point of natural evolution you must have resort to the miracle of supernatural creation." You see Mr. Haeckel is honest, and says the hypothesis of *generatio equivoco* is merely an inductive necessity, as a maxim of natural research, but it is no fact. Yes, yes, Mr. Haeckel, I would add, this is so; without the acknowledgment of vital force as a force of nature, organic life is a miracle.

Mr. Wm. Thomson went beyond Haeckel and advanced another dodge. He admits that organic matter could not at any time originate from inorganic matter, and suggests the first organic germs may have reached this earth upon meteors or aerolites, falling down upon it, after having traveled through space filled with organic germs; or those meteors may be fragments of a destroyed earth, upon which such life existed.

There are, however, too many objections to this hypothesis. The crust of the earth shows distinctly that life had a beginning on this planet; hence there is not the least ground to maintain, it had no beginning on other planets. If a beginning it had here, there, or anywhere, the question remains precisely the same, by what force? Besides the aerolites which have fallen on this earth are composed of some twenty well-known elements, mostly iron, all contained in this earth. No new element was discovered in them, and but one-third of those which compose our earth. There is no cause whatever to suppose that life came with those aerolites, which contain no other new element; or that life originated on an earth of twenty elements prior to one of sixty. Again, all meteoric stones by the velocity of their fall, if by nothing else, are encased in a molten crust, like a coat of varnish, and come in a strongly heated state; so that, if there ever had been any living germs on any, according to Pfluegner's experiment, it must have been destroyed long before it could have reached our earth.

No less unfortunate than Thomson's is Mr. Fechner's hypothesis. He thinks organic matter is its first and original form, from which inorganic matter was prepared, by fire we suppose, or as coral reefs are built up. Good, Mr. Fechner, I would say, the hypothesis is genial and novel; but we are afraid it proves too much in our favor.

If all matter was originally alive, then vital force was prior to all other natural forces, and our definition of life becomes self-evident. First all atoms were alive, hence all were controlled by vital force; then the atoms died, fire changed them into the inorganic body, then and there the other forces made their appearance, probably as mere reflexes of the vital force. The only difficulty with Mr. Fechner's hypothesis is, no means are left to prove it.

All other dodges of this kind, feeling matter, world's ether, the fall of gelatinous matter, having been declared mythical, we have arrived again at the beginning, what is life? We could close here, and insist on our definition, without fear of refutation from any scientist, as all the other hypothesis and theories prove a failure. But the matter is much too important to have it rest on a mere hypotheses. Let us seek all the truth we can ascertain on this important point, to gain an established principle of biology. Therefore, ladies and gentlemen, I invite you to my next lecture, when I hope to continue the discussion on the subject of biology.

LECTURE XIII.

BIOLOGY.—PART II.

Permit me, ladies and gentlemen to open this second lecture on biology with a passage from Shopenhaur. He says (Willen in der Natur, p. 59) "It certainly follows from my system, that every being is its own work. Nature which never lies and is naive like genius, testifies to the same, how every being merely takes the spark of life from another precisely of its own kind, and then grows up before our eyes. It takes the material from abroad, form and motion from itself, which are called growth and development. So also empirically, every being stands before us as its own work. But the language of nature is not understood, because it is too simple."

Numerous are the objections, which have been raised against this passage, and yet it is correct. It says in a metaphorical sense only: that every living being stands before us as its own work. This means, that the causes of its existence, growth, and identity are in each organism itself. Every real phenomenon must be explained by its inherent principle. It is unscientific to derive for instance, the nature and character of a man before us from the antedeluvian radiate, or from his supposed ape-like ancestor. As sure as we now speak and act as men and not as monkeys, so sure all our actions and reactions rise every time from our own constituting principle.

The same precisely is the case with every organic being. Life appears new and peculiarly individualized in every organic being. The germ only is from the parental stock, and consists of a cell or cells containing in miniature the characteristics of the parental organism and the ability of being unfolded to a free being, by the differentiated vital force. In consequence of the germ, every new organism must run through the same cycle of changes of form as its parents; and in consequence of the differentiated vital force, new characteristics appear in every new individual in a manner of apparent freedom and independence; so that no two organic beings are perfectly identical.

In objection to this theory it might be advanced, if vitality is a force, then like force in general it must be one and universal; if so its phenomena must appear everywhere with mathematical precision the same. To this, I have to say, vital force is universal and does manifest itself in identical forms everywhere, although not with mathematical precision; but it is also individualized, and in this form it appears with freedom, because it is life and not merely mechanical force moving inert matter. Let us understand these points.

That vital force is one and universal is evident by the identity of characteristic manifestations in all organic beings. All consist of cells and the various arrangements of same; hence the groundwork of life is the same in all forms, in as far as the morphotic structure of the cells is the same in all organisms, and different from crystals in three particular points: 1, The cell never produces geometrical solids, it maintains universally the globular form; 2, It does not combine homogenous elements, but chemically different substances; 3, The cell is limited in size, while the crystal is not.

Again, in all cases the young plant or animal begins its life in a small germ, runs through the three states of embryo, development and maturity, and ends in death, *i. e.* the vital force leaving the organic structure, it can offer resistance no longer to the other forces which decompose and dissolve it.

Furthermore, all organic beings live by the same internal functions of absorption, assimilation, secretion and excretion. Whether the tree absorbs inorganic matter from earth and atmosphere by its roots and leaves, to prepare its own kind of sap, on which it subsists, lives, and grows; or the animal consumes organic food passing through a chemical process in the intestines, to prepare the new blood necessary for the nutrition of that particular animal, it is always the same process of absorption and assimilation on the part of the cells which constitute that particular body. Whether the tree exhales the superfluous oxygen or the animal the superfluous carbon, and excretes the combusted material in any form, it is in all cases precisely the same process of secretion and excretion.

And lastly I will mention the universality of the sexual instinct for the preservation of the race, which manifests itself with striking similarity and equal force in all classes of organic beings.

Here are four great characteristics of life, which have nothing in common with inorganic matter and its forces, and are invariably the same from the lowest plant up through the whole series to man. The elementary structure, development, mode of subsistence, and propogation of the race are universally identical. The sameness of phenomena in all cases points directly and distinctly to one and the same cause. Although the individuals in which these phenomena appear are multitudinous, still the vital force must be one and universal.

But we see organic individuals only, each of which stands before us as its own work, manifesting a certain degree of freedom and independence in its morphotic peculiarities. We can not deny their individual existence, as little as we can doubt their dependence on the substance. Whatever philosophers may have advanced on the problem of individuation, its possibility or impossibility; it disappears before the universal fact, that the organic kingdoms exist of individuals only, each of which is, and moves around its own center. Besides, there are the following especial points, which necessitate us to recognize individual existence in the organic kingdoms.

Every organic being sustains itself by the labor of its own organism, which changes foreign matter into this particular body. Look at the tree; the cells of its roots absorb water and metal from the earth, which rise through its pores to all extremities, while the leaves inhale from the atmosphere the carbon, oxygen, and other elements; all of which are chemically changed by the organs of the tree, to a sap peculiar to this tree and necessary to its sustenance, to rise and fall in the wooden channels, and be changed to roots, stem, bark, foliage, buds, blossoms, and fruits of that particular kind, and no other. If the absorbed material undergoes not the chemical change in the tree, it kills the same. But changed by the organism, it produces here the pear, apple or plum tree, bud, blossom and fruit, there the vine, grape, and its sweet juice, here the orange and there the apricot, etc., all by the work of the tree's peculiar organs. Here is a lily, there a rose, here a violet there a narcise, so entirely different in shape. size, odor and color, all under the influence of the same light, heat and electricity, all sustained by the sap from the ground and the gases from the atmosphere. In all cases, we see the individuality of the plant with its own organs at work, to live and thrive.

Look at any animal, or rather look at man, and you have individuality perpetually manifested. Here you have a vast number of various cells in union and harmony to form the human organism. Each cell or set of cells differs materially from all others. There are brain cells, muscle cells, nerve cells, lung cells, blood cells, bone cells, etc., each of different chemical proportions. All these cells are subject to continual losses by secretion and excretion, and must be continually supplied by the blood, each with the particular chemical ingredients and in exact proportion, as required by its nature. The body stands in perpetual connection with the outer world. The exchange of materials, taking in and paying out, goes on without intermission. This restless process of breathing, feeding, and digestion, to prepare fresh blood, to roll both fresh and old in a perpetual circle to every part of the body and back to the heart, going and coming continually, changes the foreign matter of our food and inhalation, into the proper chemical material to feed and sustain every cell according to its peculiar wants, and to carry off the combusted particles, to be purified for future use or to be excreted. The human organism prepares human blood from the same material, from which the cat makes cat blood, the dog, the lion, the tiger each his own blood, simply on account of the difference in the organism. The organism itself, without any interference from abroad, carries on this perpetual and intricate process, by which it is, grows and thrives, so that the perfect individuality of every person or animal is demonstrated by its self-sustaining organism, and we have clearly before us, every being as his own work.

Individuality is manifested next in the will and the muscular motion. Every individual has a will of its own, and the muscles obey the will. I do not wish to be understood that vegetables have no will; there is will everywhere. I only wish to refer here to animal will.

Although there are certainly class instincts peculiar to entire races of animals; still there is so much variety also in these class instincts that the presence of will can hardly be doubted; and instinct itself is but steady will.— When I move my finger, lift up my hand, walk, look on, listen, or whatever change I effect, will is manifested which prompts certain muscles to the performance of mechanical labor. This will with its muscular instruments is in the individual and not outside thereof. From whatever center it may come, from an unconscious nerve center, or a conscious mind, it comes from the center of this individual and no other. Whether center or mind be affected by inner feelings or outer impulses, the will and subsequent motion are always in and by the individual itself. Mr. Darwin's theories of natural and sexual selections, if there is any truth in them, fully demonstrate will and individuality in every man, animal and plant. The volitions are so numerous that no number can express them; and yet each proceeds from some organism and not from the other, and establishes its individuality.

Next in the chain of individual and independent manifestations we come to the very limit of all natural science, as Du-Bois-Reymond calls it; we come to the fact of consciousness. I do not refer here to the wonderful self-consciousness of the reasoning man; I merely refer to the conciousness of the lowest or highest animals. It feels cold or warm, pain or pleasure, sees red or blue, extensions or forms, hears sounds and distinguishes them, tastes sour or bitter, smells pleasant or offensive, and is conscious that it feels, sees, hears, tastes, or smells so and not otherwise, and is conscious of its own individuality. All physical forces do not account for the simplest sensation much less for the consciousness thereof, and least of all for the necessary reflection, I am conscious, hence I am an individual, and none can feel, see, hear, tastes or smell for me. No body can participate in my pain or pleasure; he can only sympathize with me, if he has experienced similar feelings in his own consciousness. So we know *a priori* that each individual is a thing complete and independent in itself.

Last, but not least in this review of facts, we come to the influence of emotions on each particular organism.—Gladness, success, happiness, quicken the circulation of the blood, accelerate the digestion and increase the process of assimilation. Sorrow, fear. disappointment, anxiety, perished hopes, undermined prospects, discouraging aspects, etc., exercise a detrimental influence upon the organism, and not unfrequently ruin the constitution. A false friend deserts me, I sit and mourn, hate to eat or drink, the blood courses slower through the veins. A dear friend dies, grief overcomes me and culminates in a delirious fever. I love hopelessly, and my heart's blood is consumed. I am wronged, dishonored, neglected, deserted, forlorn, I feel repentance, remorse or shame; and it undermines my health and ruins my constitution. Who will describe the numerous and various cases of persons, pining away in painful emotions, or being enlivened by gladness or happiness; or how differently these various emotions effect different persons and different animals? None can, because, there is freedom and independence in every organism. It all depends on the individual and independent of all persons and friends.

Here then is individuality in the self-sustaining organism, will, consciousness, cause and effect of the emotions; and each characteristic of individuality is a manifestation of individual freedom and independence. Therefore vital force is not only one and universal but also individual, hence my definition of life is established in fact. It is no hypothesis, it is the theory suggested by the heterogeneous facts.

At the same time, it is proved that vital force is a reality, an immaterial substance. Life had a beginning on this globe. It could originally and can now manifest itself through the cell only, and by the unification and harmonization thereof; hence there must exist a force to bring forth and to govern organic matter and organic beings. That agent being at the same time one and universal, differentiated and individualized, say like electricity in the galvanic battery insulated on a glass plate; it must be an immaterial force, which can be separated from the matter in which it operates. It can not be the mere function of the organism, for it is in the cell, it is alike in the most different organisms, it is one and universal, it can be separated from the organism. It is no heritage, because every being stands before us as its own work.—
It is in fact, because it governs matter and forces in the preservation of the organic individual's identity. It is not a conglomeration or complex of forces, because it produces effects, such as assimilation, production, will, consciousness, and emotion, in which none of the known physical forces are detectable. Hence it is a peculiar force. Can any naturalist, scientist, chemist, physicist, or philosopher tell us, why we should not call it vital force? If none can, and so I do varily believe, then my thesis is established, and we have a solid fundament of biology.

If this is so, then this universe is no piece of dead mechanism. There is vital force, there is life in it. Force is not only immaterial but also alive. Here begins another aspect of ontology. There is life. We live because there is life. So we have gained a third and very important point. We have now mind, force, and life three realities to lead us into the province of teleology, and metaphysics. Ladies and gentlemen we have crossed the threshold in the temple of pure cognition and higher knowledge. Let us go on upward, upward, to the utmost limit of human capacity.

> "The mind of man in this world's true dimension
> And knowledge in the measure of the mind;
> And as the mind in her vast comprehension.
> Contains more words than all the world can find.
> So knowledge does itself far more extend.
> Than all the minds of man can comprehend."

> "A climbing height it is, without a head,
> Depth without bottom, way without and end;
> A circle with no vine environed,
> Nor comprehend, all it comprehends.
> Worth infinite yet satisfies no mind,
> Till it that infinite, of the Godhead find."

LECTURE XIV.

THE ORIGIN OF SPECIES.

LADIES AND GENTLEMEN—How did the numerous species of vegetables and animals come into existence? This problem of biology or cosmology has become very important in philosophy, and has engaged human intelligence of the highest order to solve it satisfactorily. Besides the existing Flora and Fauna, we have before us three instructive volumes, compiled by the maker of all things in the beginning, in characters universally legible, to be interpreted by the disciples of science, from which we ascertain the origin of species. These three volumes are, the crust of the earth with its fossils, the ocean teeming with life, and the embryonic phases which every living being has to pass before it becomes an independent individual. Whatever we read not in either or all of these volumes concerning the origin of species, we know not; and all the facts read therein are susceptible of a variety of explanations. Therefore we have now three theories on the origin of species, to which I may be permitted to add a fourth.

The theory first in importance is that of Mr. Charles Darwin, an improvement on those of Carus, Goethe, Lamarck, Geoffroy and others, by an addition of a number of hypotheses, apparently combined to a system of evolution, or actually a theory of transmutation. This theory starts out with the hypothesis that originally organic life, in its lowest forms, was started on this globe in one or more typical beings, whatever their number, morphic and physiological structures were—Mr. Darwin is silent on these points—gifted with the latent capacity of unlimited variability, fit to adapt themselves to any condition in ocean, land and atmosphere, by the acquisition of new organs and the useful adaptation of those possessed, to maintain themselves under all changes of conditions, in the combat of existence, *i. e.*, against inimical influences of the elements, and hostile concurrents for subsistance and females. Those creatures which failed in the adaptation or the combat, either remained in the lower classes of organisms, or were destroyed by those of better adaptation, more force or skill in the combat of existence. These organs, internal or external, acquired by adaptation were, by another hypothesis, inheritable, if useful, which is called the hypothesis of descendency, resting upon the other hypothesis of natural selection, resting again upon the facts of domestic selection in a few instances. To all these hypotheses comes one more, called the law of correlation, a law, a something without a name or definition, which in case of the useful adaptation of one or more organs to new conditions, made permanent by descendancy, changes and re-adjusts the whole organism in harmony with the acquired organs, instincts and organic process. If, for instance, a graminivorous animal, by a change of conditions, would be forced to subsist on animal food, its teeth would adapt themselves accordingly. This change would become constant (for which, however, no proof exists) by descendency; and by the law of correlation the stomach and the other intestines would be changed and re-adjusted in correspondence with the teeth. This morphic transformation and transubstantiation would involve also a change of appetites and instincts, and all the physiological changes of bones, muscles, nerves, size, shape, color, hair, wool, feathers, or bark.

It must be borne in mind that in this theory there are united the hypotheses of unknown creation of the first types, unlimited variability, combat of existence, descendency, and the law of correlation, none of which is supported by facts, and all of which must continually co-operate to produce new species. Every one of those hypotheses, however, has been refuted by Naegeli, Baumgartner, Wigand, Lange, Von Hartman and others.

The second theory is that of Mr. Baumgartner. He starts from the law, "*Omne vivum ex ovo, omne ovum ex ovaria.*" Our knowledge of life reaches not beyond the egg, or germ cell; hence the origin of species must have its discernable cause in the egg of the ovary of the living organism; and there he supposes to find it by heterogeneous generation, or the metamorphosis of germs; *i. e.*, it is in the nature of the organism that, from time to time, one or more of any type produce eggs, or germ cells, of an advanced type, which then becomes constant. So the development progressed from type to type, from species to species, genus and variety, by the periodical metamorphosis of germs. Such heterogeneous generation is actually found in nature, but not beyond the production of varieties, never to produce species. In this case we have first the beginning of life on this globe as a fact, a miracle, an unknown and unknowable anomaly, so that the hen must have preceded the egg for evermore. In the second place we have the same unwarranted leap to a far-fetched conclusion, as in Darwin's theory. Mr. Darwin says, because in domestic breeding certain useful organs are made more useful, and this is inheritable to a certain extent, therefore nature must do the same thing universally and continually, although domestic breeding is premeditated, never succeeds beyond slight variety, and can not be made constant in all cases. Mr. Baumgartner says, because a metamorphosis of germs, as an exception and mostly among the lowest class, occurs, productive of varieties, therefore nature must do the same thing universally and continually, and so produce species. Both conclusions are illegitimate. Both Darwin and Baumgartner take the hypothesis of unlimited variability for granted without the slightest evidence, and the assumed law of correlation without any definition. Both theories are conglomerates of hypotheses and auxiliaries, none of which has been or could be supported by scientific evidence.

The third theory is that of Mr. Wigand, the great botanist, and most forcible opponent of Darwinism. He advances the creation of type cells or type protoplasma, in which all the capacities and abilities of the species, morphic, anatomical and physiological, together with all the instincts and appetites of each organism, were originally packed and stored away, to be developed and brought in use in millions of years, under the changes, convulsions, catastrophes and new conditions of land, sea and atmosphere. This is a mere hypothesis, of course, which admits of no scientific evidence, as we possess no means of obtaining any of those type cells or protoplasma, or to ascertain their inherent force, if we could procure them.

Each of these three theories, taken for granted, it is maintained, will account for the origin of species; consequently, the facts which have a bearing upon this problem must be susceptible of a variety of explanations; and so they are, as the scientific adherents to any of these theories amply prove. Again: none of these theories accounts, or begins to account, for the origin of life on this globe; while each of them, aside of all other agencies, must resort, and does resort, to an organic force which is extra-organic before it can become organic. I prove this so:—

Cuvier, Flourens, Agassiz, Pictet, Humboldt, and others maintain that within the bounds of human knowledge of historic and prehistoric ages, no change of type or species has been noticed. Pictures of animals upon Egyptian obelisks, brought to ancient Rome; animal mummies brought from Egypt, and an investigation by Cuvier concerning the Ibis then and now, as well as the elephants found in northern ice-fields, fully testify that no change whatever has taken place in those animals. The sheep, goat, ox, ass, and camel were the same domestic animals in the time of Father Abraham as they are now. Wheat taken out of an Egyptian grave was sown and the same wheat which we possess now was reaped. The same cereals and fruits on which man and beast subsist now, are noticed without change through all pages of history. The plants which Passalaqua has found in Egyptian graves, as described by Knuth, the botanist, are identical with ours, although some varieties have been lost, it appears. Hence, within historical ages, there is no trace of unlimited variability, and looking beyond that, Agassiz well remarked, that the polyps building up the reefs of Florida for at least 30,000 years, are still the same polyps precisely.

As far as the existing Flora and Fauna are concerned, unlimited variability is not discernable; therefore, if this was the case in previous stages, it ceased to exist with the constant types before us; hence they are the resultants of former developments, from the infusorium and algæ up to man and the cedar of the Lebanon. Had this evolution been effected by mechanical means, it must have been very slow and gradual, with all gradations and transition forms from species to species. But that is exactly not the case; there is no systematic chain of organisms on earth. Not mere fissures but gaps which can not be bridged over, separate the species in numerous instances, so that Mr. Carus supposed the links missing on this earth must be somewhere in the moon or in the planets, from which the earth was separated.

The same precisely is the case with the fossils. The testimony of evolution is imbedded in the crust of the earth, but not evolution by any mechanical means; for there also the transition forms are missing, and no trace of genetic unity is left. This is admitted on all hands.

But then the Darwinists say, what we have not discovered yet we may discover hereafter; for all we know such transition forms may exist and be discovered any time. To this, however, we could well reply, whenever you will have made those discoveries, then we will take them into consideration, for which we have no cause now, as that which might be proves nothing in science. As far as our knowledge reaches now, the factors of evolution are not, and were at no time, of a mechanical nature. But we have a better reply than that—the ocean and the embryo prove that such transition forms never existed, hence can never be discovered. In the ocean we have before us the original and primary generation, from the protoplasm at the bottom of the sea, up to the great monsters of the deep. In thick, warm, salt water, the generation of organic beings took its start; thus much is certain, and continuous production, propagation and extinction of life went on undisturbed and uninterrupted. The ocean was not exposed to the violent eruptions and catastrophes as was the land; hence, in the ocean the original picture of organic creation is preserved intact. A thorough knowledge of oceanic biology is equal to the best information we can obtain of the first work of organic creation. But there, and there again, the fragmentary character in the system of organisms, without specimens of transition from species to species.

The same is the case in embryology. Our knowledge of the various stages of the embryo from actual observations is very limited, because it is too difficult to make them among higher animals. Yet it is maintained that the embryo runs through all phases of organisms as its ancestors did in their natural development from species to species. Then this ideal semblance of those various stages to certain animals is converted into a proof, that the higher organism must have evolved from those lower organisms, which it represents at different times, as though an ideal semblance was any proof of genetic unity, and more than an ideal semblance was certainly never discovered in any embryo.

The analogies, in the best known cases, are far-fetched, and the conclusions based thereon are very doubtful, to say the least. But granted they are not, in order to argue from the standpoint of the Darwinists, they prove again the gaps and breaks in the systematic chain of generation by evolution; for the embryo runs only through a few stages, and offers no points of transition from species to species, or genus to genus. It runs, after all, only through the stages of known animals, and the unknown must remain unknown. Consequently, there are no such transition forms, none will ever be discovered, and evolution can not be established on mechanical principles.

Besides, only the Darwinists attempt to account for the origin of species by mechanical agencies. Mr. Wigand begins with an organic force which makes type cells or protoplasma. Mr. Baumgartner knows of organic force only throughout the whole process. The same is the case where Mr. Darwin speaks for himself.

Sexual selection and the ornaments acquired to this purpose, spring from no mechanical principle. It is instinctive, connected with a choice, directed to an object, consequently it is will and intellect connected with an appreciation of the beautiful, neither of which can be reduced to mechanical principles. Again : if descendency is altogether mechanical—which I can not see—the law of correlation is entirely psychical and altogether independent of the organism. What is the law of correlation? A principle or force which works a change, physiological and morphic, in the whole body, because the one or the other member thereof has been changed by mechanical causes.

This morphic change, however, depends on the causative force, a force which must be active everywhere and at all times to effect this re-adjustment; without it, the whole theory falls to the ground, and with it, we have before us a psychical principle as the main cause of evolution. As nothing can be its own cause, the animal itself is not the cause of the law of correlation. As this phenomenon is universal, so must be the cause, which in many cases must work simultaneously on several individuals, which stand in no connection with each other, as for instance the peculiar appendages of an insect, and the flower from which it seeks its nutriment.

Therefore, when we speak of an organic force, we can not refer to something which is in this or that plant or animal only ; or to anything which this or that organism produces. When we say force, we certainly mean something which produces phenomena, and not a phenomenon produced ; we mean something causative, and not something passive. The organic force which is the cause of evolution, must be extra-organic, cosmic, vital force. If Darwin, Baumgartner and Wigand, must admit, and do admit, directly or indirectly, our first principle of biology, viz., the cosmic existence of vital force—or is there anybody who can tell the difference between organic force and vital force?—and with their respective theories they can not account for the origin of species, and the origin of life on this globe, and I can, starting from the same principle; then my theory, which makes the fourth, is certainly preferable to the three former, especially as it includes their main points in their proper places. Let us hear this fourth theory.

Evolution and differentiation as the fundamental laws of creation are now admitted on all sides, and Mr. Haeckel well remarks, that they are fundamental in the Biblical cosmogony. Differentiation signifies the individuation of beings from and by the universal substance; and evolution in this connection signifies the systematic and rising succession of organisms from the lowest to the highest in the process of individuation. The substance is psychical. Matter is known to us only in the form of incoherent and heterogeneous elements, which, if not united by an active force, must remain apart forever. Matter retains in all forms that negative quality of dissolving in its elements, if not prevented by active force. Whether matter itself be created or uncreated, is indifferent here; the first act of creation of this or any other planet was the action of a central force upon inert and homogeneous elements, in counteraction of their negative quality of separation, to subject them to the creative and forming principle. This central force, from which all forces in matter are materialized derivatives, is a function of the substance which is will, intellect, life, God, and partakes of the same nature precisely, *i. e.*, it is not only psychical; it is will, intellect, life. It is an effect, and must, in its *quodity*, be like its cause. Vital force, which is also will and intellect, is the central force of this and every other planet. It appears as the unconscious planetary soul, if you wish to call it so, in its materialized state, and remains mind under all conditions, will, intellect, and life. It overcomes inert matter, prevents its dissolution in heteregeneous elements, and stands in perpetual relation to and in harmony with itself in all planets and suns, according to its own eternal laws. It is perpetually and continuously at work to govern matter, and to liberate itself from matter, to become itself again, *i. e.*, conscious and self-conscious, in individualized lives. Its first success in this direction is the production of the protoplasm in the depth of the sea. This is *generatio equivoca*, although science can neither imitate nor explain it; still, if vital force is the central force, then the miracle is explained. Protoplasma are little, very minute building-stones, from which vital force constructs all organisms in the whole system of life. These protoplasma may have lived thousands of years in the depth of the ocean, before matter was so far under the control of vital force, to unite some of them and form a cell; for a cell is already an artistical structure. Now thousands of years life may have existed in cells only, and uncountable millions of them must have perished before matter was so far under the control of vital force, and sufficiently qualified to serve as material to the building up of organisms; for organic beings are made of organic matter, and subsist on organic matter. Also the vegetable requires organic matter for its subsistence; hence countless millions of protoplasma must have preceded the cells, and countless millions of cells must have preceded the lowest organism to qualify matter for organic purposes. The cells are the building material for the vital force. They do not give character to the organism, nor can they produce any; the organism gives character to each of them in the various beings and the various members of each. Therefore Wigand's hypothesis of type protoplasma or type cells is false and unnecessary to explain the origin of species.

Organic matter, as far as we know, is just as indestructible and unchangeable as metallic matter. Notwithstanding the continual work of death and decay, organic matter remains in its compound condition upon the earth's crust and in the waters of the ocean as well as the bottom thereof. It is continually increasing by the very labor of the organisms, changing inorganic into organic matter. Every plant or animal that dies adds to the bulk of organic matter, and renders higher conditions of organism possible. Therefore after a sufficient bulk of animal matter had been laid up in the household of nature, and vital force, as the formal principle, had advanced to the organization of the perfect cell, that force could now bring forth everywhere, as the state of the ocean, land and atmosphere admitted, organisms adapted to each age and condition of the earth and its various parts. The efficient cause of the first organisms was not in the cell; it was cosmic in the vital force, which weaves cells and destroys them to increase its material for more and higher organisms; hence the first organic types did not spring from the cell or cells by the combat for existence, subsistence, and females, not by natural selection, descendency or otherwise mechanically. When vital force had succeeded in reaching the next highest step in forming the germ cell, the egg, it had also material enough accumulated to develop the germs into organic beings of different individual characters under different states of ocean, land and atmosphere, with sufficient material left to provide for organic beings, organic food preceding them in time, as it were, to prove design and premeditation.

We know that nature loves variety. It loves to exhaust all possible forms. There are type metals, type crystals, type infusoria, and in no case any of Darwin's or Baumgartner's supposed causes could have been co-operative; why should not the same central force of nature have, in the same manner and by the same cause, produced type vegetables, type animals, species and races of all kinds? None can see the necessity of either Darwin's or Baumgartner's theory and hypotheses.

Besides all this, if you run up and down the whole organism, you will find that all centers in man. Man is the complex of the entire organism that has come to our knowledge; and all parts of all organisms are harmonized and perfected in man. When the fathers imagined a higher order of beings, viz.: the angels with wings, because man is debarred of these organs of the bird, they did not take into consideration that human hands controled by human mind are far superior to wings. The whole organism consists of various divisions of the human organism among various species of vegetables and animals. Therefore modern biologists succeed so well in discovering physiological and morphic semblances between parts of man and parts of this or that animal, but they will never succeed in discovering the human organism in any animal. If we take the fact as it is before us, it simply teaches that the central force had to run through all these various phases of organisms, as expounded above, before it could realize itself in the self-conscious center called man. That there are leaps and gaps in the system is simply because the species have no genetic relations—they are all ideal, and ideal only. The evolutions were not external, they were internal in nature, with their cause in the vital force, hence in perpetual connection with the whole of nature, and especially this ocean, land and atmosphere; which were by no means systematic in their various formations, in our sense of mechanical system. The crust of the earth is full of violent transitions, eruptions, catastrophies, sudden revolutions without systematic connection with previous conditions.

This fourth theory admitted, viz.: that the cause of evolution is in the internality and not in the externality of nature, in the vital force itself, and not in the morphic structures it produces, in the psychical substance and not in matter, then the facts advanced by Darwin, Baumgartner, Wigand and the others, fit it very well. Nature, or rather its central force, may have employed all those means, combat for existence, natural selection, variability, descendency, correlation, heterogeneous generation, metamorphosis of germs, and a hundred other means, psychological or mechanical, under different states, circumstances and combinations of influences, external or internal, to reach its object and to realize itself, although neither or all of these auxiliary means account for the origin of species, and the appearance of man on earth as the complex of the whole organism.

It must be remarked here that Mr. Darwin, in regard to the combat of existence to obtain females and sustenance, has overtaxed his imagination. The equal number of male and female births, a universally acknowledged fact, was left out of the account. Evidently this factor must be dropped in the vegetable kingdom and among monogamous animals, as most of them are. Among birds and pigeons especially, the birth of one male and one female of each brood at the time is the rule, and the pair will stay together and propagate, if not separated by violence. Among polygamous animals my observations and experiments have taught me, that those of one breed will keep together in peace, and the males divide the females among themselves by common consent. Combats among animals on this account are very rare, except where the females are destroyed by the hands of men, and also then they are limited to a very short time annually, so that in reality the whole factor amounts to very little.

Mr. Darwin appears to imagine this earth, land and ocean, as rather a small patch, overstocked from the beginning by a vast number of living beings, with scanty provisions of food made for them, so that the combat for subsistence was perpetual. On our real earth, however, after so many thousand years of increase in the animal kingdom, the soil still offers plenty for the support of all, and not one half of it can be used yet. There it an affluence and superabundance in nature, which Mr. Darwin evidently did not take into fair consideration, or else he could not possibly have laid so much stress on the combat for subsistence. All the traceable effect this factor may have produced is, that the weaker members of a race or species may have been thrown back from the original center of the family. This is actually the case among men, and undoubtedly also among animals. The earth always was large and rich enough for the animals, for they were not tied down to one spot as man was by agriculture and despotism. The animals migrated freely.

The fourth theory accounts for the appearance of life on this globe and its progress by evolution to the constant types before us, provided it can be proved, which I will attempt, that there is will, intellect, system and design in this universe, outside of all organic beings. This leads us into the question of teleology, to be discussed next.

We have arrived at the inner court of the sanctum of philosophy, duly cleansed of many prejudices, and lawfully prepared to open the sealed book of efficient and final causes, on which all questions of religion, moral government, education, the whole fabric of society depends.

LECTURE XV.

ON TELEOLOGY.

LADIES AND GENTLEMEN.—We begin this evening to speak on Teleology, the end, aim and object of the things in nature, and of nature itself. The word *telos*, end, aim, purpose, or object, was introduced in philosophy by Aristotle, and I use the term teleology in this sense, as most German writers do, and John StuartMill partly did; although the word has been used differently by theologians and scholastic philosophers. What is the object of all these things? what is the end and aim of the whole world of existence? why is it? what purpose is in all this? These are questions which every thinking man must have proposed to himself, some time or another. Do all things exist merely to be, to change, and to disappear, or must they fulfill another destiny, serve other purposes, and reach other ends and aims? Does all nature exist to and for itself, because it must, or is purpose in its existence? These are the main questions, to be discussed in teleology.

Some naturalists, and materialists especially are opposed to teleology, because, chiefly, it has proved damaging to the progress of the natural sciences. Lord Bacon has started this idea, and Baruch Spinoza has built his system on efficient causes exclusively. God and nature have no ends or aims in view, according to Spinoza. Still naturalists like Bergmann, Leuchart, Milne Edwards, Eschricht, Von Baer, Fechner, Agassiz, and others, and philosophers like Leibnitz, Kant, Trendlenburg, and Lotze have admitted the inevitable necessity of teleology in philosophy, and its utility as a maxim of research.

The main causes of this difference of opinion are these: Teleological speculations were pressed too far and too much in the detail, so that they became ridiculous, and nugatory to science. The philosophers, and especially in France maintained to know the ends and utility of every object in nature. When Chrysipp advanced, the horse was made to draw wagons and the ox to drag the plough, he did not know that the horse may be used in the plough. When it was maintained, the Negro was born to be the slave of the white man, or nations exist for the support of thrones and their occupants, the teleology was evidently false. When others insisted upon, that the beautiful colors in the vegetable and animal kingdoms served no other purpose besides pleasing the eyes of man the teleology was one-sided. When others completely turned the order of things, and said the bird's feet have been constructed so by a benign providence, in order to enable them to roost upon the branches of the trees, protected against many a danger; or the teeth and intestines of the carnivorous animal were so constructed by an All-wise Creator, to enable the animal to subsist on the flesh of others, they only proved their utter misunderstanding of the teleological idea. Therefore Mr. Holbach said, "Those who discover beneficial ends everywhere, are like the lover who sees nothing but perfection in the object of of his affections." Let us add thereto, and those who see every where the want of beneficial ends are like hypochondriacs who will never be pleased.

Besides some of those enthusiastic thinkers, instead of seeking to discover the causes of phenomena and to ascertain the laws thereof, as science should and must proceed, ingeniously guessed the utility and ends of natural objects and their qualities, and called their guess work science, as Mr. Darwin often does. Still it can not be maintained, that science should exclude all teleology, as we know it has led and leads to many valuable discoveries, as Mr. Darwin often proves. Mr. Cuvier had so well studied the teleology of organism, that finding one petrified tooth of a fossil animal, he constructed the whole animal accordingly, and gave rise to a new science. He discovered almost mathematical certainty in the relation of the bones to each other in the same body, so that one bone or a part thereof, or even a tooth, sufficed him, to build up the whole animal as it must have lived.

The next cause of difference in opinion was the anthropomorphous conceptions of God and nature. The household of nature was looked upon like a human family affair, God and nature were made human in theory and practice, and then the utility and ends of all natural objects were expounded from that standpoint; so everything must have its knowable end, there must be no waste in nature, there must be nothing too much and nothing lacking any where, every being must be happy in its sphere, exactly as a wise man would arrange his household affairs. God and nature were measured by the narrow guage of human wisdom and, as a matter of course, were found wanting. There is, however, in nature an incalculable waste and perpetual destruction of life.— There is, in the realm of nature, pain, suffering, misery, destruction, and death, as well as joy, pleasure, happiness, and goodness, and pessimism is entitled to the philosopher's most earnest reflection. Still, all of this entitles none to the conclusion, that there is no plan, no design, no grand object, no final cause or causes in nature. It rather suggests to every reasoner that, in order to construct a satisfactory teleology, the anthropomorphous conceptions of God and nature must be dropped. God is no man and nature no dame, and the household of nature must be measured objectively, by the facts which it presents, and not by our feelings, wishes, hopes, desires, or prejudices.

The last objection to teleology is purely materialistic. The materialists want no final causes, no ends, aims, designs or purposes in nature; because they want a dead universe, a lifeless, loveless, and thoughtless piece of mechanism, a self-moving, self-sustaining, and self-adjusting automaton, like Mr. Huxley's man, without any God, anthropomorphous or absolute. But as soon as you speak of ends, aims, designs, or purposes in nature, they say, you must pre-suppose an intellect in or above nature; an intellect which designs and executes, hence an almighty and supreme intelligence, which is God, whether called by this or any other name; the very thing which those materialists do not wish to admit.

As a maxim of natural research it may do, *i.e.*, we may purposely close our eyes to the spiritual or intellectual side of nature, in order to see clearer its mechanical side and better understand these laws. But in philosophy, it will certainly not do. We must see both sides; if possible we must view the whole to arrive at the truth. Therefore we must discuss teleology.

The most general and least holding ground of gross materialists is, they will not admit the existence of anything not perceived and not perceivable by our senses. Then they say, if there was an intellect in or above this nature, why is it imperceptible? We answer first with a passage from the book of Job:

"But wisdom, whence shall it be found? and where is the place of understanding? Man knows not its price; nor is it found in the land of the living. The deep saith: It is not in me; and the sea saith: It is not with me.— Choice gold shall not be given in exchange for it; nor shall silver be weighed for its price. It can not be weighed with gold of Ophir, with the precious onyx and sapphire. Gold and glass shall not be compared with it, nor vessels of fine gold be an exchange for it. Corals and chrystal shall not be named; and the possession of wisdom is more than pearls. The topaz of Ethiopia shall not be compared with it; it shall not be weighed with pure gold.

"But wisdom, whence comes it? and where is the place of understanding? since it is hidden from the eyes of all living, and covered from the fowls of heaven. Destruction and death say: with our ears have we heard the fame of it. God understands the way to it, and He knows the place of it. For He, to the ends of the earth He looks; and He sees under the whole heaven: to make the weight for the wind; and He meted out the waters by measure. When He made a decree for the rain, and a track for the thunders' flash; then He saw, and He declared it; He established it, yea and searched it out. And to man He said: Behold, the fear of the Lord, that is wisdom; and to depart from evil is understanding."

Job in this beautiful poem simply says, I see intelligence everywhere, but I can not understand the essense of this powerful medium underlying, regulating and governing all things. We know, that nothing is perceptible to our senses *per se*. Matter is imperceptible, until the influence of forces render it perceptible to human senses. Force is imperceptible until it manifests itself in matter. We know force and matter exist, but we also know that our senses perceive them not in a state of isolation; hence we surely know, human senses can perceive matter or force by and in their combined manifestations only. We know them, each and all by induction. We certainly know just as well and by the same method the existence of intellect in or above nature.

We hear the words, or examine into the deeds of intelligent beings; we weigh the ideas thus presented on the scales of our judgment, and decide, intelligence is the cause, words and works the effect. We can not perceive the intellect, "It is hidden from the eyes of all living." as force without matter or matter without force. When the Bible states that God said to Moses, "No man can see me and live," we may add, no man can perceive with his senses, intellect, intelligence, force, or even matter unless under the influence of force.

And yet, who can deny its existence, and assert there is no intellect? While he admits or denies, he acts under its influence; without it he can do neither. While I now speak and you listen, not to the mere sound of words, but to ideas, definitions, theses, arguments, and conclusions, intelligence stands in perpetual report to intelligence by the mediation of articulate sounds and auditory organs, ganglia, and brain fibres, all moved by the intellect.— Here it is in this very moment, and yet we see it not, can not perceive it with our senses, not even imagine it. Our knowledge necessitates us to acknowledge three substrata of essence, viz: matter, force and mind or intellect, each of which is imperceptible in its isolation; and on the universal law: "Nothing can be changed without a cause external thereto influencing it," we must maintain that the changes in matter, force, or mind from the imperceptible to the perceptible are caused by reciprocal causation.

Still it is no more difficult to comprehend the nature and substantiality of the intellect than of any force at work in the realm of nature. Force is immaterial hence psychical, so is the intellect. Force is a susbtratum of things, so is the intellect the substratum of all thoughts and their monumental objectivity. Force becomes known and perceptible to man by its manifestations in matter, so does the intellect in words and works which are its manifestations. You can not imagine matter without force, so you can not imagine thoughts, words, and mental works without intellect. There can be no machine at work without propelling force, no motion without motive power, no music without a musician, no resultants without a substantial cause. We know certainly as much of the nature and substantiality of the intellect, this no rational materialist will deny, as we do know of the nature and substantiality of force.

I maintain, we know more and better of the intellect than of the forces in general. We know the manifestations of forces by the effects exercised on our organism, when we have become conscious thereof by the mediation of the iutellect. Hence all knowledge of force is with us *a posteriori*. We have an indirect knowledge thereof.— Our intelligence, however, is in our consciousness directly, not carried into it by any agency whatever. Every person is conscious of his own intellect; hence every one knows its existence, nature and substantiality *a priori*, directly and with the utmost certainty possible.

Illustrate so: I am certain of the presence of artificial heat in this temple, by the sensation I feel different from what I felt outside of the building. I am conscious of this sensation by my intellect. Still this is not certain, for the temperature of the atmosphere or of my body may have changed meanwhile, and I imagine artificial heat where there is none. But there can be no doubt to me, that I am now in this temple, because I know it by no agency outside of my own intellect. The objects outside of myself undoubtedly are, although I possess in myself their images and ideas only. I could not imagine or think them, if they were not. The image presupposes an original, the idea a suggesting object; but after all and with all the ingenious arguments and formulations by Ueberweg and Czolbe, my knowledge of all things outside of me is indirect, *a posteriori;* therefore the imperfection, the error, the combinations of phantasy to be corrected by the intelligence. This is certainly not the case with man's intellect; I know myself *a priori*; I and my intellect are identical, hence my knowledge of it is the most certain I possess. All which must be proved in teleology, concerning the intellect, is its existence and substantiality outside of man.

Having taken the first bulwark of materialism, let us open on the second. Force in nature is regulated by law, *i.e.*, under given circumstances it manifests itself so and always, produces these and no other effects. This constancy of cause and effect, established by experience and experiment, is the law of the force under consideration.— The laws of nature are the laws of forces. So, for instance, we know as universal law that heat rises, or heat expands. Once knowing the law of a force or cause, intelligence reverses the order, to discover the cause from the effect or effects before it. Illustrate so: We know heat expands. Seeing the mercury rise in the thermometer, we conclude, the heat increased, for there is more expansion, or seeing the mercury fall, we conclude, there is less heat now in the same locality.

Here is synthetical truth *a priori*: Every phenomenon in nature is the effect of a cause, and every cause is subject to its law, upon which all structures of science and philosophy are reared. It is the law of causality. All naturalists, mathematicians and philosophers must submit to it, or rather each of them starts from it. There is no effect without its cause, no cause without its law.

This truth is, first, in the human intellect spontaneously. Since man exists, he has sought cause behind each effect, although he did not always succeed in finding the correct one; and has always expected the same effects from the same cause. He always must have considered this law universal, it must be in the intellect. Experience teaches the law of isolated cases, its universality is spontaneous in the intellect. None can think of a human intellect in unobstructed activity without this synthetical truth, which is one of its attributes, manifested in the lowest as in the highest processes of reason. Therefore intellect and law of causality are inseparable. Preyer maintains: "That (the knowledge of) causality is an original capacity of the understanding, prior to all experience, and an *a priori* category, has been known already to Kant. That this is the only category, this cognition of Schopenhauer, is probably the greatest philosophical progress since Kant.' Helmholz also adopts this theory.

This truth is, secondly in all nature outside of the human intellect, confirmed by all human knowledge, observation, experience, and experiments, as far as science has penetrated into the mysteries of existence. Here is already something universal in nature outside of the human intellect, which is also in it, the law of causality, and it is the essentiality and motor power of both. This law in man is in his intellect and inseparable from it; hence this same law in nature outside of man must be in an intellect.— Well then, here we have already an intellect in nature outside of man. Still we do not wish to achieve so easily so important a victory over materialism, especially as its champions wish to be met on their own battle ground. Let us try again.

The law of causality being admitted, we all agree, that nothing in this universe stands above or beyond the law. But as the forces and elements are heterogenous, and each follows its own law or laws, still the universe, as far as we know, is one in order and harmony, the forces of nature must either converge to the one single purpose of sustaining permanently this order and harmony, or one superior force must control all of them, or else there must be continual conflicts in nature among elements and forces, which we know not to be the case. Consequently there is co-operation, co-ordination, and sub-ordination in nature, which is its law of laws, or force of forces.

Illustrate so: All parts constituting a body, be it a man, a bird, a house, a factory, an earth, or a sun, must be harmonious in their co-ordination and sub-ordination, and thus co-operate continually, to make the existence of that respective body possible. If a wheel or screw in a machine is not constructed according to the law governing the whole machine, the order and harmony thereof is destroyed. If the heart of a human being be too large, or his stomach too small relatively, according to the law governing his whole organism, then the order and harmony thereof is destroyed. It is universally so, although each part of every body be governed by its own laws, the whole as a unit must be governed by a superior force, or the various forces must converge in this one particular point of sustaining intact that particular unit or body.

Here then is teleology, here are final causes. In every unit you may single out in this universe, infusorium or man, fungus or palm tree, crystal or sun, there is final cause before you, there is teleology, there is end, aim purpose, and design. And if you then rise from the individual objects to the universe as a unit, you have before you always the same teleology, the same, end, aim, purpose, and design of preserving the whole intact as a harmonious unit. There is the same final cause in the grand totality of nature as in every minute object thereof.

Here then is final cause and final causes. We leave it to the materialists to decide, as they please, whether these ends and aims are reached by the converging nature of all forces, to meet at these teleological centers, or whether one superior force governs the others and directs them to this end; and take them by their own word: " Where there is end, aim, purpose, design, teleological center or centers, there must be intellect to design and execute ;" this intellect in or above nature must be allmighty and allwise, and can only be called God, that very God whom they wish to strike out from the nomenclature of science and philosophy.

But I am not going to accept this important conclusion on the authority of materialism. Having now laid out the basis of teleology, I will examine into the particulars, to convince you, that there is just cause for every honest thinker, to adhere to teleological and theistical philosophy, upon the very shoulders of science and all its brilliant achievments.

LECTURE XVI.

WILL AND INTELLECT IN NATURE.

LADIES AND GENTLEMEN.—Let us look upon the subject of teleology from a reversed standpoint. Let us see whether we can not discover will and intellect in nature by the strictly inductive method, and in full harmony with natural science. If we succeed in this point, then let us say there is no will without an aim, and no intellect without design and purpose; hence if there is in nature, outside of man, will and intellect, there are end, aim, design, and purpose; there is teleology.

Seeking to find in nature, if possible, will and intellect, means we investigate whether there are any facts in nature which necessitate reason to acknowledge the existence of will and intellect independent of man; for to prove, means to necessitate reason by logical conclusion, to accept as a fact one naturally contained in another and acknowledged fact. Therefore, although knowing, as we do already, that every object of nature as well as the cosmos itself is a teleological center, and represents end, aim, purpose, design, and proper execution, consequently there must be an intellect at work in this nature, or above it, so that we might justly maintain we have continually before us the manifestations of intellect in the universe; we discover behind all objects an efficient and intellectual cause to select and apply proper means for carrying into effect ends, aims, designs, and purposes pre-established; Still we have no clear idea of will and intellect themselves, which we know now by conclusions only, and not by their own criteria; and of whatever we have no clear idea by its own criteria in our intelligence that has not for us the force of certainty and necessity. Let us make the attempt to form clear ideas of will and intellect in nature independent of man.

In our lecture on biology, we have seen that vital force

differentiated always manifests, more or less, a certain degree of freedom. Therefore, no two plants, and no two branches, leaves, blossoms, or fruits of the same plant are actually identical; each manifests some difference by which it is distinguished from all others of its kind.

It hardly need be said that this is the case, only more so, among animals, especially of the higher types, no two of which are exactly identical. The higher you rise in the scale of organism, the more conspicuous are these characteristic differences in individuals of the same race or family, so that among us Caucasians the approximate identity of any two persons, also twin brothers or sisters, has never been established. The higher the vital force rises in its differentiation, the closer it approaches fixed individuality, and it reaches it in the highest types of humanity. In the origin of species, the lower types are in a state of mutability and variability, while the highest ones are individually fixed.

The repeated assertions of modern fatalism, concerning iron necessity in nature, as though man was incapable of governing and directing matter and force, subjecting and applying them to his purposes—are entirely false if applied to the organic kingdoms, in which, as in vital force, general laws and individual freedom are observable everywhere. All objects existing according to their inherent laws, are free, the law makes them free. Freedom is limited by outer violence only. All nature and every individual thereof is free, where no disturbance from outer violence takes place. In consequence of universal freedom, the individual possesses the inherent power to deviate from the general law; and in consequence of this inherent power of deviation, no two individuals are exactly alike; the man who trains fleas to perform on a sheet of white linen, knows one flea from another, as we know one rose from another by the appearance of tints and arrangement of leavlets, also without the aid of the microscope. So freedom is visible everywhere also to the naked eye. Let us now examine what is freedom substantially.

I define, freedom is the actualization of an inherent will. There can be no freedom without a will, and in every act of freedom which is actualized, will is the cause and freedom the effect. Therefore it is certain that in the two realms of organisms, will is actualized and manifested in every individual thereof; therefore, it must be there inherently and permanently. One need not adopt the whole dogma of Schopenhauer, viz., will is the world's substance; or even refer to E. von Hartmann's elaboration.

of the dogma, and must still see the presence of will in the manifestations of freedom.

Is not this anthropomorphous speculation? Do we not transfer our human will to animals and plants? The Darwinists can certainly not raise such an objection to our proposition, for with Mr. Darwin the origin of species depends entirely on the presence of will in every individual of the two kingdoms of organisms. The ornaments and improved songs of the male bird, for instance, are purposely acquired to please and captivate the attention of the female; which demonstrates will. Prehensile organs and defensive appendages grow out of the animal's body, according to Darwinism, by the repeated exertions of the animal's will. In fact, the whole system of Darwinian evolution is based upon the principle of teleology, carried into every detail or organism, always tacitly postulating the presence of active will in every organic individual. If we could accept Darwinism as an established fact, teleology and the existence of will would be proved *eo ispo*. Therefore if the Darwinists subscribe not to Schopenhauer's dogma—*i. e.*, will is the worlds substance—they must anyhow admit its inherent and permanent existence in every organic being.

But aside of Darwinism, the proposition is demonstrable by facts of actual observation, as Schopenhauer and Hartmann have done. Cast a glance upon the center in the organic chain. If a glass of water containing a polyp be so placed that the vessel be partly in the shade, the polyp will instantly move to the sunny side. The little creature exercises its will to abide under the influence of the sunbeams. Put a living infusorium into the glass within a few lines of the polyp and it will agitate the water so as to bring the infusorium to its mouth and swallow it. Put a dead infusorium, or another small object, in the same position to the polyp, and it will not move.— Here is the exercise of intentional will. It is no rare instance that two polyps fight over an infusorium, or that an Australian ant cut in two, the two halves of the same body will fight one another to death or exhaustion. Here is will under the impulse of an affect, will without brain, ganglia, or nerves. As you rise in the scale of organism the manifestation of will becomes so much more perceptible to the cursory observer. The dog wills to follow its master. The horse wills, or wills not, to perform its task. The mule is stubborn; the lamb is gentle; the lion, like the cat, patiently watches its prey and an opportunity to seize it. It is will in all these instances, perceptible to the naked eye.

Will, outside of the purely human will, points directly to the existence of the following conditions. There must be in the animal a natural necessity to be gratified, and this necessity must produce a corresponding desire. This desire is called instinct. Then the object outside the animal and within its limits of perception, calculated to gratify that desire, by an instinctive impulse, agitates and intensifies the desire to an actual voilition. So the will is moved and volition produced by an inward impulse and an outward motive. It combines the efficient and final causes, is at the same time subjective and objective, viz: in its origin and object. The volition must always have in view an object, to be reached by adequate means or exertions. While desire and impulse rousing the will to volition, are purely instinctive, the volition employing means to reach a given end, must be intellectual.

Will in every instance of volition can be intellectual only, so that none can possibly think of will or volition without an intellectual process. Therefore will and intellect, as also Hartman maintains, are inseparably united.

Illustrate so: The dog is hungry, feels the natural desire for food. A piece of meat, which he sees or smells, gives him the impulse to gratify his desire by this particular piece of meat. Here the instinct stops. He wiils that piece of meat, *i. e.*, he employs the adequate means to overcome all obstacles and reach his aim. Suppose a person be in the room whom the dog fears, he waits for that person's departure, and as soon as this has taken place, the dog snatches the meat and carries it to a quiet corner. This is certainly an intellectual process. In any and every case of animal actualization of will in volition, the same process exactly takes place; for means must be chosen, adapted to an end; a purpose is to be realized. Although not every volition is realized, and the means employed are not adequate in every instance, still the intellectual process is always the same, as the means must be present to the animal before the volition is executed.

.Without entering here again upon the difference of human and animal will and intellect, we are entitled to the conclusion that there is will and intellect wherever there is life. Reflex motions, falsely called reflex will, being involuntary motions of the muscles caused by external irritations, are no acts of will. They are mechanical and find their cause in the peculiar construction of the muscle; but every other motion is certainly the demonstration of will and intellect.

It must be added that the animal's natural desires, appetites, etc., called instincts, are the resultants of muscular motion, contraction, and expansion, purely mechanical and beyond the control of animal will or intellect.— Those mechanical processes which we call instincts are the works of apparatuses teleologically constructed to sustain the animal and the race, without the continual co-operation of which the animal can not live. These involuntary actions of the body, as the actions of the heart, stomach, and intestines, which act as levers to the will and intellect, are all minutely regular, systematical and teleological. Being the causes of the instincts, they also are regular, systematical, and teleological. Therefore the instincts are fundamental principles of teleological centers. All of them, although beyond the control of the animal, nevertheless harmoniously co-operate to work out one final cause, viz.: the existence of the individual and its race. No animal can have a superfluous instinct, nor can it have one less than necessary to its purposes, as the instincts spring from the involuntary muscular action.— So the mechanical and involuntary actions of animal and vegetable and the resultant instincts show distinctly end, aim, purpose, and design, and consequently will and intellect in nature outside not only of man, but of both organic kingdoms. Therefore Kant maintained that the instincts are revelations of Diety.

Are will and intellect substances, or are they accidents attributes or functions of a substance? The foolish idea that life, will and intellect are accidents of the organism, has been refuted already, for we have proved before the existence of vital force, and have shown already that the organism is the resultant of will and intellect; it is a teleological center. Nothing can be resultant of itself. Besides we know will and intellect exist in the invertebrate animals down to polyp, and by the demonstration of freedom we discovered them also in the vegetable kingdom; hence they are independent of nerves, ganglia, brain, and every particular arrangement in any organism.

We know that will and intellect exist and manifest themselves wherever life exists, as we know that light and heat, positive and negative electricity are in constant connection. Life itself is known to us as a psychical substance, called vital force. Hence will and intellect are either in constant unison with life as independent agencies, or they are the attributes of life, or *vice versa*.

Again we know that a substance not always manifests all its attributes simultaneously. For instance, heat consumes, expands, and is the cause of the flame; yet, under certain conditions, heat manifests not its burning and flaming properties, and under other conditions, its expanding property remains latent. So we know that under certain conditions, like sleep, disease, idiocy, somnambulism, etc., life appears without will and intellect at that particular time and space, consequently we are entitled to the conclusion that will and intellect are attributes of life, *i. e.*, vital force is the substance, will and intellect its attributes. Inasmuch, however, as the attribute is that, to speak with Spinoza, which reason understands of the substance as being its essence; vital force is, besides its other attributes, will and intellect; or intellect is will and life; or will is life and intellect; the three are one substance, manifesting itself in its various attributes. It is no triune substance or a trinity, as a substance can be one only, but these three manifestations, as appearing to the human intelligence, are in fact only three attributes.

We have seen in our lectures on biology that vital force is both universal and differentiated. It is universal because a force, and differentiated in the individual beings. It is omnipresent in its universality, and appears in time in its differentiation. Hence we know beyond a doubt or peradventure, the existence, substantiality, and universality of life, will and intellect in this vast domain of nature, in man and outside of him, in animal and plant and independent of them, here and everywhere, now and forever; since the attributes can not be separated from the substance of which they are attributes, as little as extension can be separated from space. Life being a substantial force outside of all beings, will and intellect must be.

We consider our thesis established; hence freedom, life, will and intellect in nature outside of man and all organisms; therefore, also, end, aim, purpose and design, there is teleology in this vast domain of the universe.

Upon the broad highway of the natural sciences and under the steady guidance of induction, we have arrived already at the very gate of metaphysics. But we shall not yet enter it as long as other proofs are at our command to overthrow the bulwarks of materialism, and to establish the spiritual and intellectual side of nature.— In our next lecture we will try another standpoint, and see whether it leads not to the same results precisely.

LECTURE XVII.

SUPERHUMAN WILL AND INTELLECT IN HISTORY.

LADIES AND GENTLEMEN.—The history of the human family is a continuation of the grand scheme, realized in the creation of this earth, and the host thereon. Creation's closing work was man, and with the first man history begins, to end with the last. Although we have no exact knowledge of its earliest details, still we know that the development of facts, which underlie the pyramid of history, begins with the doings of the first man, and not with the mollusks or opossums. The first human deed was the first stone at the base of the towering structure called history.

The law of causality, the continual chain of cause and effect, is as clearly and intelligibly manifested in history, as in physical nature; not, indeed, in brain dispositions and improved nerves, but in deeds and facts of actualized mind outside of the human being. So, for instance, the late Franco-German war was certainly not the effect of particular brain dispositions newly acquired, for wars were waged thousands of years ago; still it was the effect of causes, and became in its turn the cause of the French republic and the secularization of the Papal dominion, the further effects of which are now incalculable; all, however without any changes in brain dispositions or structure of the nerves.

Those who have read Herder, Kant, Guizot, Buckel, and others on the philosophy of history, Hegel on the history of philosophy, or Steinthal's and Lazarus' essays and books on the *Vœlkerpsychologie* (psychology of nations), will certainly not deny the law of causality in man's history; and I believe, the materialists also will admit, there is sufficient ground to rely on those authors in this particular point.

Is there teleology, final cause in history? is end, aim, object, design, purpose and proper execution discernible in the history of man, or is the human family drifting upon the boundless ocean of existence without any ultimate purpose? If there is teleology in history, then the question arises, by which force or forces, power or powers? It is evident to my mind, that there is teleology in history and by a superhuman power, and I will expound to you the evidence in my possession.

We may set down as a general principle: Every continuous chain of cause and effect in nature is teleological, resulting continually in teleological centers, which every individual being is. What German philosophers call a *causalnexus* is also a teleological center, the final cause of the complex of co-operative efficient causes, to bring forth this natural object, crystal or sun, protoplasm or man.— Their successive co operation proves the primary intention of the process. What is true in nature must also be true in history. The same chain of cause and effect must also be teleological; and each state of society, every day, every hour, and at every place, must be a teleological center. Analogy is certainly in my favor, and logic no less. For every state of society, being demonstrably the result of preceding efficient causes, is the ultimatum in the logical chain of legitimate conclusions, always the only logical result of all preceding links, and contained in them. So the very last effect at any given time, is the very aim and object, or final cause, of all preceding causes and effects, down to the primary cause, and must be contained therein potentially and intentionally, because logical in each and all. This is certainly premeditated teleology in the strictest sense of the term. Each state of society, in its turn, becomes again the cause of the succeeding one, and so on to the supposed end of history; hence the whole chain is logical and teleological.

Let us suppose, we see two piles of square stones on opposite sides of a street. We imagine some purpose or another, although not the correct one. Artizans take apart the square stones on one side of the street and erect a gothic cathedral with its ornamented doors, windows, steeples, and emblems. On the other side, other artizans take apart the other stone pile, and erect from the well-measured square stones a Byzantine temple with its doors, windows, pillars, arabesques, and minarets. Now we are able to tell that in two seemingly equal piles of stones, there were actually two complete designs of two different structures. Having this point we run back through every step of the previous proceedings to the first men who met and schemed the erection of these buildings, a perfect chain of cause and effect with its teleological center now visible in the two buildings, although the very buildings must have been present potentially all along in every step taken, and every piece of work done. Then we calculate the influence to be exercised from those buildings on the human family, which leads us not only onward but also backward to causes, which produced in the Christian the taste for the Gothic style and in the Jew a predeliction for the Oriental style of architecture; and how the ideas connected with this point reached our generation and will influence coming ones, all in a logical chain of cause and effect.

Take another point to illustrate: Here I stand before you to exercise the privilege of free thought and free speech. We call this a final cause, a teleological center of importance in history. This privilege is a resultant of preceding active causes. The Hebrew polity had to pass through a series of reforms made possible by the advanced spirit of the age, which is again a resultant of other and ever as many causes, while the freedom of speech and thought is the offspring of the American revolution. This again is the child of previous causes, among them the stamp act, duty on tea, the conduct of George III, and his advisers, the situation and the disposition of the colonists, the bravery and patriotism of George Washington and his compatriots; none of these causes could be omitted and the same end be reached. All this, however, depends again on previous conditions of the pioneers in Europe, and the discovery of America. Go back a little further, America could not have been discovered, if there had not risen, in the fifteenth century, a nameless and aimless passion among maritime nations for discoveries. The passion would not have taken hold upon intelligent men, if the sciences, especially mathematics and astronomy, had not been previously improved, and together with the astrolab applied to navigation. These improvements were caused by Moors and Jews. It is all one chain of cause and effect, and the last effect, as now my speaking to you, must have been contained potentially in the very first cause and in every following effect, which in its turn again became a cause; and every state of society between the two ends, at every time and locality, was a final cause, a teleological center. As little, indeed, as the artizans could have erected the two different buildings from the two piles of stone, if the previous and efficient causes had not been embodied therein, intentionally and premeditated; so little could I now speak before you here, as I do if those numerous efficient causes had not preceded this final cause, or if it had not been contained in all its efficient causes. It is a *causalnexus*, therefore it is teleological center.

Therefore, in our day, no philosophical historiographer writes history otherwise than on the teleological principle, which the Germans call *pragmatisch*; because history as a chaos of disconnected events like bubbles on the surface of a boiling ocean of chance and casualty, always bursting to give way to new bubbles, is as unintelligible as indifferentiated matter in its zero state with no forces moving and shaping it. The great object of the student of history is to know the facts correctly and in their teleological connection with the whole structure of history.

Well then, if history is teleological, and its progress depends not on brain dispositions and improved nerves by descendency, then it is actualized mind, human, extrahuman, or both.

It has been affirmed in a previous lecture, that history contains the monuments of actualized human mind. Although man is not absolutely free, as he is no absolute being, still he is free to a certain extent, as we know both empirically and *a priori*. Every being in nature is free, as long as it exists in harmony with its inherent laws and without disturbance from abroad. Every organic being, we have seen, manifests will, intellect and freedom. With his will, intellect, and freedom, there can be no doubt, man makes history, *i.e.*, he seizes, in every generation and clime, the opportunities and advantages before him, adds to them his experiences and inventions for the use and benefit of himself, his fellow-man, and posterity. It is man's exclusive privilege to make history, because he and he only connects in his mind past, present and future; only he feels the necessity of improving, because he alone is idealistic; and the desire of benefiting others living with or after him, because he alone is a moral being. His selfishness can not overcome entirely his ideality and moral nature, and the social structure is so, that the happiness of the individual, to a great extent, depends on the well-being of society. All this is certainly true in general, although the rule is subject to numerous exceptions.

But having admitted already the law of causality, it must also be admitted that man can not make history by his will and intellect exclusively; he must be in harmony with that law which is superior to man's will and intellect, as the whole is superior to any of its parts. The human family consists of individuals, and not of an indifferentiated or consolidated body; hence mankind is subject to that law, as well as every individual, with the freedom of regarding or disregarding that law. Therefore, in the whole course of history, as in the whole process of nature, there is universal necessity and individual freedom. If thousands, or nations rebel against the law, they must stand the consequences; but other thousands and other nations will obey it and reap its benefits. The mystery of successful statesmanship and prophecy is honesty of purpose, a thorough knowledge and appreciation of this law. This law of causality in history is certainly extrahuman. Organic nature offers the following analogy:

Every egg of every fish, and every seed of every plant, possesses the inherent will to become an organic being of its own kind, and must become one, if left to its inherent law and will. But there is an extra-organic law, which, as it regulates the equal proportion of male and female births, or the increased birth of sound and strong male children after wars and epidemics, or the regular progression of births and deaths in the various generations, also regulates the proportional increase of fish and plant of each kind in the natural state, that there exist so many, no more and no less, at any given time and locality. The numerous eggs and seeds are necessary to reach that end surely, all destructive agencies otherwise necessary taken into consideration. Without the will of the fishegg there can be no fish, nor can there be one contrary to that extraorganic law. So man's will, though free, is subject to that extra-human will of causality, as far as history is concerned. Let us call this law the Logos of History, and ascertain its general principles.

There is perpetual progression in history from lower to higher conditions, exactly as in this earth's creation.—There are breaks, violent catastrophes and eruptions in the earth's crust, and there are also in history apparently illogical, bloody, and disturbing eruptions, cessations and retrogressions, momentarily and locally; but in the totality of history, the progression from lower to higher conditions is perpetual, incessant, and logical. Yet human nature is the same forever in all its fundamental qualities. Our modern Anglo-Franco-German thinkers certainly stand no higher in the scale of intelligence than the Hebrew prophets of old. Our reasoning powers surpass not the men of ancient Greece or Rome. The ideals of art are no loftier now than they were in classical ages. Not in quality, but in quantity, of experience and inventions, utilized, generalized, and popularized, the progression of history is manifested. The child now is precisely the same as were those born when the Egpptian pyramids were erected. Now it sees, hears, and learns more than it could then; the material increased and spread, the methods and facilities of instruction have been improved. Take twin brothers to-day, place one in a metropolis and the other in a solitary farm house, and you will see at once the whole difference.

Mankind not progressive in quality, and still the progression in history steady, the principle of progression must be extra human, and the first general principle of the Logos of History must be: It preserves, utilizes, and promulgates all that is good, true and useful, and neutralizes all that is wicked, false and useless or nugatory;. exactly as the extra-organic will and intellect works in the organic kingdoms. Let us cast a glance upon history.

Pharaoh and the Egyptians oppressed and enslaved the Hebrews, who possessed traditionally certain ethical truths. The consequence is the departure from Egypt, the legislation in the wilderness, the establishment of a new civilization in Canaan, the rise of the prophets, the promulgation of monotheism and its ethics, powerful levers in the world's civilzation. The Egyptians opposed all this; the Hebrews were against it, the Logos of History preserved and prompted, shaped and directed, and Moses had a perfect right to say God had sent him.

Alexander crossed the Hellespont to subjugate Asia to the Macedonian scepter, and died in Babylon a young man; his whole family vanish; Western Asia is the heir of Grecian literature and science, a new civilization springs up, and Egypt under her Ptolemeys becomes again the center of culture, to give rise to a new phase in the world's history, which neither Greek nor Barbarian designed or wanted, and the Logos of History turns evil into good to preserve, and to progress.

A mad king of Syria, Antiochus Epiphanes, in need of much money and good sense, determines upon apostatising the few millions of Jews in Palestine. The rebellion follows, ends with an independent government under the Maccabean princes; and decides forever the superiority of the Hebrew monotheism and ethics over Greco-Roman speculation and mythology. Pompey and his host meddle into the affairs of the Jews, two centuries of incessant combat ensue, which brings the Jews into Italy, Spain, France, Germany, and also to the East, and with them comes the death of Heathenism in Europe, Arabia, and

Persia. Rome subjects Jerusalem and loses her gods.—Every step in the process is extra-human, although all done by men.

But we need not go back so far; the illustration is right before us. If the queen of Spain in 1492 could have guessed the consequences of the voyage by Columbus, that he would discover a new world, where the coffin should be made for all crowns and scepters, America would not have been discovered. If the clergy of those days had supposed that this would be the land of religious liberty, free thought and free speech, no human being would have been permitted to leave Europe and seek these shores. They can not accuse any man or any body of men in particular to have been guilty of making this new world a new starting point in history, to revolutionize all former conceptions of public government, social and political rights and privileges, classes and divisions; to change the entire status of labor and the laboring man by new conceptions and inventions. It is all one chain of teleological events, conducted by the Logos of History, to find its conceivable final cause in the universal and democratic republic.

Take another side of the picture. If Pius IX., had known in 1848 that his siding with the so-called legitimate princes, the despots of Europe and their tools, when the spirit of revolution like a hurricane swept over the continent, would cost him his temporal power only a quarter of a century thereafter, and could have convinced himself that the two dogmas of immaculate conception and infallibility, and the forcible acquisition of the boy Mortara for the Church, would estrange so many hearts from the Church and embitter so many thousands against her dominion,—no kaiser and no Bismarck, no Victor Emanuel and no Garibaldi, could have dethroned him, united Italy, or broken down the power of the Jesuits.

Again, if the then three kaisers of Europe could have thought that the late German-French war would build up the French republic, which if granted two decades of peace will necessarily republicanize Europe to the very gates of Constantinople and St. Petersburg,—the war would not have been waged, and a Napoleon would still play comedy in France. You see, no Bismarck, no kaiser, no Pope, nor any body else, has brought about those remarkable changes in history which transpired in our very days and under our eyes, as it were. It is all extra-human; it is the Logos of History that rights the wrongs, turns the course of events in favor of progression in spite of all the wickedness of rulers or nations, preserves the elements of truth, goodness, and usefulness, to be shaped in new events, and neutralizes falsehoods, wickedness, all that is useless or nugatory.

So in all ages of history large masses were blindly moved by an invisible power, to achieve worthless purposes in barbarous and bloody wars and rebellions; but the Logos of History always utilized the human blood and misery for the cause of progression. Great men, like King Saul, were troubled with evil spirits, committed unpardonable follies and barbarous outrages; the Logos of History sends those actors to oblivion, renders their work harmless, and turns it round for the benefit of progressive humanity. Mephistopheles himself, who always wills the bad, must serve good purposes. In the grand drama of history there is no evil; and also in this particular point history is identical with the great household of nature. There is no devil.

But it is time for me to close. I can not finish my subject in one lecture. I propose to complete it in my next.

LECTURE XVIII.

SUPERHUMAN WILL AND INTELLECT IN HISTORY CONCLUDED.

LADIES AND GENTLEMEN.—The Logos of History manifests its extra-human existence also in the inevitable punishment of national sins. As nature, everywhere and inexorably, punishes every transgression against the physical laws, so the Logos of History dispenses just retribution for national misdeeds. The words of Isaiah might be written upon every public building: "If ye be willing and obedient, ye shall eat the good of the land, but if ye refuse and rebel, ye shall be devoured with the sword; for the mouth of the Lord hath spoken it."

From the distant Orient, the terrible goddess whose name is Nemesis, came to the Greeks who worshiped her with awe; and the Romans erected her a temple in the capitol among the superior gods. What Isaiah expressed in intelligible words, mythology represented by the symbolic goddess; the principle of retribution and retaliation, enforced by an invisible power, is the foundation of both and deeply seated in the consciousness of all nations and tribes. The Pagan Jethro said to Moses: "Now I know that Jehovah is greater than all the gods; for the very thing which they used wickedly came upon them," (the Egyptians, as a retribution.)

It is not as clearly manifested in the life of the individual, and may not be enforced as rigidly; but nations, history and consciousness agree, live, grow, and flourish on their virtues; suffer, decline, or perish of their vices, and all that by agencies perfectly natural, though controlled by super-human causes.

The Bible and the history of Israel are full not only of the most terrible warnings to this effect, but also of telling facts in corroboration of this doctrine. The student of ancient history knows full well, how mighty empires forced together by the sword, established in blood, and held under the subjection of terror, were crushed under their own terrible weight, by an invisible power mightier then despots, heroes and armies. Awe inspiring ruins of impregnable castles, proud, wealthy, and populous metropoles tell the tale of Nemesis' inexorable execution. Begotten in bloody wrongs, fed by injustice, and nourished with human blood and tears, they fell fat victims of raging vices. So ended Assyria, Babylonia, and Medo-Persia; so perished the Roman Empire, and in the beginning of this century also its successor, the Germanic empire.

Look for a moment at old Germany with her outrageous crimes, committed for centuries on burgher, peasant, Jew, bondsman, and foreigner, all of whom were mere sheep, cheap commodities, marching chattles, worthless trinkets, superfluous dregs, filling space for the special benefit of so-called noble-men, priests, soldiers, and their task-masters called public officers and executioners; committed also on Italy, Spain, the Netherlands, Poland, and other Sclavonic countries trampled down by German armies.— Look upon her history and you will find, how her sons were slain by the millions, first in the internal feuds of knightly ruffians, and in the various, bloody crusades, then in Italy, Turkey, Spain, France, and the Netherlands, next in Fratricidal rebellions, the Thirty and Seven years wars; so that she was at no time without war, till at the beginning of this century she fell down dead at the feet of Napoleon and France, dead from crime and exhaustion, and there laid for nearly seventy years a helpless giant, a byword among nations, trampeled upon by a thousand petulant despots, ridiculed and despised by Metternich and Nesselrode first, by Napoleon and Cavour then. Strange analogy! Like the Hebrews of old, Germany had her seventy years captivity, to expiate her national sins, and to send forth into the world her sons, bearers of ideas shipwrecked at home, under the blind captaincy of mad despots.

Next in crime and retribution, among the modern nations, is certainly France which, since the closing decade of the last century has been expiating her enormous sins by currents of blood. And next to her, only in crime more atrocious and in vice more hideous, is awful Spain, whose sins are as old as her history, and as grievious as those of Sodom and Gomorrah. Every inch of her soil is drenched with innocent blood, and her atmosphere is ripe with the sighs and groans of human beings who expired under diabolic tortures. In the Netherlands and the West Indies, in Mexico, and Peru, in Naples and Sicily, she has insatiably swallowed human gore and destroyed human happiness. Behold now, how she wades and swims in her own blood, how her sons exterminate one another, and yet there is no peace to the wicked. So the Logos of History avenges the outrages committed by nations and, although long suffering, surely visits the iniquities of parents on children and children's children to the third and fourth generation of those who abide in wickedness.

But we need not go so far to conceive evident manifestations of the Logos of History punishing national sins. Up to the year 1840 the people of these United States lived on the virtues and wisdom of its sires. Then it began to grow fat and to kick. Its first crime was going to war with Mexico. War is always a crime, for one party must be in the wrong, most usually both are. The principle of settling difficulties by war is in itself a crime. War of conquest is a barbarous crime on humanity, every life sacrificed is willful and malicious murder on the record of a nation. War of a republic against a sister republic is the extreme of all national crimes. And yet the United States waged war upon the Republic of Mexico, which ended with the annexation of California and New Mexico.

Please, look upon the consequences. Gold, plenty of gold and silver were found in the annexed territory, more than in all central Europe; but we have a depreciated paper currency, and the precious metal disappears mysteriously under our hands. We owe more money in Europe than any nation ever did outside of its boundaries. We are the richest and poorest people in the world. We have plenty of the precious metals, but for the last fifteen years none for our own use; and the interest we pay to foreign purses consumes the fat of the land and makes the heaviest tribute ever paid by any vanquished nation. Before we had all that precious metal, we had a few less millionaires in this country, but many, many less poverty stricken persons and beggars, less corruption, and less crime in proportion. The increase of the precious metals, however vast and out of all proportion, has done us no good. It is ill-gotten wealth. It is the fruit of a national crime. The Logos of History avenges the wrong, and threatens to sacrifice the liberties of this people to a few millionaires and avaricious hirelings.

Yes, Mexico was conquered and we triumphed. But the infatuation was still on our brains, when lo, the threatening demon of dissension with its flaming torch, in the year 1849, set the whole country on fire which burnt on and on until the conflagration of the great rebellion threatened to consume the whole land. Over the acquired territory, the admission of California into the Union, the dissension broke out, the balance of power among the States was thus disturbed, and the quarrel ceased no more. Now loomed up the old sin, slavery, and together with the new one filled the measure of iniquity to the brim; the Logos of History appeared as the Nemesis of retribution, and behold the ten thousands of victims, to exipate for our national crimes.

How wonderful, how marvelous! While we expiated our sins by our blood, the French invaded Mexico to strangle the republic (this was the beginning of Napoleons end and Bazaine's shame); and we were offered the opportunity of making atonement to Mexico. William H. Seward, who manœuvered three emperors out of this continent, did make that atonement, and assisted in the restoration of the Mexican republic. So that debt was canceled. But among us at home the offended Logos of History is not appeased yet. Corruption in high places, an insatiable avarice among public men, public robbery in all shapes and forms, the dominion of ignorant masses over the intelligent in many States, the consequent oppression and military dictation, financial ruination and despondency in private circles, the heaviest burdens of taxes ever paid by a people, are only a few of the consequences under which we groan now. But I need not produce any more to convince impartial men how, before and under our very eyes, the Logos of History manifests its extra-human existence and activity by the inevitable punishment of national sins. True, the means are all human, all natural as cause and effect; but the first cause which employs those means to reach these ends, and shapes all teleologically to produce these final causes, is certainly extra-human.

The sure punishment of national sins can not be denied, as history and the consciousness of man speak too londly thereof. No nation inflicts wilfully a punishment upon itself, and yet it comes. It comes without any man's design or intention. It comes by a teleological arrangement of events of particular fitness. Therefore it must come from the extra-human Logos of History, which as far as nations are concerned, is certainly sovereign and immutable justice.

"*Die Weltgeschichte ist das Weltgericht*"—In the world's history is the world's judgment day.

The next phenomenon in which the Logos of History manifests itself is most extraordinary; its name is Genius.

The existence of genius and its appearance at the right place and time is as mysterious as the center of the universe. Genius is the superior spontaneity of the mind in productive and executive powers. It conceives, not by an act of volition or tiresome reflection, but freely, generously, and unsolicited; it conceives finished and complete thoughts, schemes, designs or images of universal truth, irresistible impulses to execute or realize, utter and promulgate. All this comes like a flash of lightning, unawares and not expected, in words, symbols, visions, or finished thoughts. The ancient Hebrews called it *Ruach hak-kodesh*, "a holy spirit," and modern language names it Genius.

Talent is not genius. Talent discovers, and genius invents. Talent thoughtfully connects, combines, and unites; the work of genius springs forth from the mind in one solid cast, like Minerva from the brain of Jupiter, complete and harmonious. Talent trims its productions for the public mart, and modifies them to suit its customers; it depends on outward circumstances. Genius is inconsiderate, self-relying, and, like unconscious beauty, without any intention to please. Talent wills, and genius must: it is an internal necessity. Talent is local, genius universal. Talents are acquired, and genius is inborn. The ancient Hebrews looked upon the men of genius as special messengers from on high; therefore the Psalmist sings: "Ye shall not touch my Messiahs, not mal-treat my prophets," which is recast in the New Testament thus; "A sin against the holy ghost will not be forgiven." (with special reference to Deut., xviii. 18, 19.)

Wherever genius is placed it manifests itself by breaking through the crystalized forms, and pouring forth new creations of the mind, and is therefore, the cause of all progressions in history. It is the same genius under all circumstances, although its peculiar manifestations always depend on outer circumstances. It is the same genius, whether among peasants or mechanics, students or poets, painters, sculptors or architects, in the army, in the legislature or executive council of a nation, in a school-master's chair or a composer's study. Its peculiar manifestations only depend on outward circumstances to throw it upon this or that department of human activity; but it will show every where its inventive force and the universality of its character. It is the highest differentiation of the vital force. The same genius which became a prophet in Israel, because the nation's general turn of mind was religious ethical, might have become an apostle of the fine

arts, or formal philosophy in Greece, or become a great statesman or soldier in Rome, a prominent legislator in England, or a successful inventor in this country; simply by the change of external elements giving direction to gen ius, which remains the same genius under all influences,
  Genius is not inherited. All the great geniuses whose names history gratefully recorded, stood alone, without a duplicate in their respective genealogies. We know next to nothing of the ancestors or descendents of Moses, Isaiah, Socrates, Plato, Aristotle, Homer Æschylus, Sophocles, Shakspeare, Raphael, Correggio, Mozart, Beethoven, or Hirshel and Frauenhof. The son of Solomon was a fool, and the son of Schiller is a rough hunter. Spinoza, Leibnitz, Newton, Kant, and George Washington died childless. Dante, Tasso, Milton, Racine, Lessing, and Goethe left no scion like them; Cæsar, Napoleon, like Cyrus and Alexander, left no heir of genius behind. Genius is a special commission from the Logos of History to advance the human family to higher conditions of existence.
  Most every genius works against his own will and interests; ninety-nine out of each hundred are unhappy and dissatisfied—many miserable, wretched. They feel keener, love profounder, know better, hope and scheme loftier, expect more, are disappointed and mortified more frequently, find less pleasure in carnal enjoyments than the generality of people. In consequence of their creative powers they are always at war with existing and stereotyped forms and institutions, consequently in perpetual conflict with the conservative element and selfish motives. But there is in genius that irresistible force; it must—it must pour out the truth conceived, the beauty felt, the goodness admired, careless of all consequences. Therefore the ten thousand martyrs in all departments of mental and moral creations whose places in history, marked red with blood and tears, are awfully sublime.
  And yet if it were not for the large conservative element, there could be no order, no stability, at any time; the human family, so to say, could not digest and assimilate the food offered to the public stomach. And yet, if it were not for those poor, visionary, and eccentric victims, those dreaming idealists, the men of genius, pressing onward and forward, society would stagnate, congeal, crystalize or petrify; progress would be impossible and civilization a farce on the African pattern. Genius is the leaven in the chaos of humanity, the mighty lever to roll on the inert, plump, and helpless ball.
  And yet genius is wanting nowhere, when needed.-

Every great time begets its great men, every great cause its inspired apostles. They rise, as it were, from the atmosphere of the generation which requires their energies. When the oppression of the Hebrews in Egypt had reached an intolerable degree, Moses was a man already, prepared to redeem them. In a wonderful manner, none can account for it, the 18th century brought forth a mighty phalanx of brilliant geniuses, warriors, statesmen, poets, authors, composers, philosophers, scientists, and an unconscious passion for freedom and progression seized upon multitudes, to open widely the flood-gates of intelligence, to pour in its currents upon the 19th century, the age of radical revolution, where the lowest rapidly becomes the highest, and the highest sinks down lowest, to rejuvenate the human family.

And now reason comes in and asks, by whom is this marvelous and harmonious arrangement made? In the case of genius, we have evidently before us the same universal law which governs the organic world. Plenty of geniuses are perpetually born, and all are at work somehow and somewhere, so that, all destructive agencies otherwise necessary taken into consideration, there must appear the right man in the right place, where the Logos of History wants him, to shine forth in his pristine glory, and do the pre-ordained work. The other men of genius, like the superfluous fish-egg, also perform a task; it takes many hands to build a city. Here we have before us an extra-human agency.

The law of history is progressive, and man not only remains in quality always the same, but the vast majority is conservative and opposed to every progressive step.— Yet history preserves all that is good, true, and useful, continually increases its stock, spreads, utilizes and promulgates it, contrary to the will of the masses, and in spite of all egotism and prevailing stupidity. Again in spite of all, whatever is false, erroneous, wicked, nugatory, or useless is overcome in history, by the very errors and blunders of great men and great nations; by the indomitable and irresistable Nemesis with all her mysterious furies, making war upon all corruption and degradation, and hurling continually the nugatory element and its creatures into oblivion. In spite, I repeat, in spite of all conservatism and egotism, genius rises always and everywhere, to be on hand at the proper time and place, to beget the grand wealth of new truths, to press onward and forward the inert bulk of humanity, tears or smiles, love or hatred, lakes of blood or streams of milk and honey, triumph or defeat, praise or scorn, crowns or gallows, it matters not to genius, it sacrifices itself against its own will, that then from its very blood, armed and buckled champions of the new ideas rise, to grasp the banner trodden in the dust, and unfurl it again for victory and progression; but onward, always onward is the watchword.

And yet no man schemes it, none does it with forethought and conscious design, it is all contrary to human will and prediction, still done by human agency. Who designs this grand and marvelous drama of history, chooses the actors, shifts the scenes and conducts its execution, if man does not do, not will, not contemplate it? There is but one answer to which reason is necessitated; and this is the Logos of History does it in its invisible, silent and ever efficient power, and this Logos of History is not only extra-human, it is super-human, becauses it designs shapes, and puts into execution the destinies of all men and all generations, it presides over man, and all must submit to its laws.

And now human reason turns upon gross materialism and says: "Here is teleology in history, to deny it is madness. Here is end, aim, design, purpose, and proper execution, not by one or all men, but independent of all.— There must be will and intellect extra-human, superhuman, universal and bound to no organism. It is identical in its laws with the extra-organic will and intellect in nature, hence both, are one and the same spiritual force. All your construction of atoms and atomic forces will positively not account for the existence of one sensation, much less for the grand drama of history; and the last resort, after all, is the existence of an extra-mundane spirit, as far as matter is concerned, which is no more unknowable than force or matter. Whether this superhuman life, freedom, will, intellect, and justice, universal and differentiated is a mere force, or the force of all forces; whether we are entitled to call it Nature's God, we will investigate in our next lecture, on metaphysics.

LECTURE XIX.

ON METAPHYSICS.—I. GOD IN NATURE.

LADIES AND GENTLEMEN.—In eighteen lectures previous to this we have been guided through the labyrinth of nature and history by induction solely and exclusively. We have examined facts and attempted to expound them within the bounds of the law of causality. The result of this investigation was unraveled to our cognition, wheels within wheels in the marvelous mechanism of nature and history; facts which stand behind this world of sensual realities as their efficient and final causes. The main fruit of our researches is the existence and substantiality of a force in nature which is life, freedom, will, and intellect, and also government and justice in man's history, universal and super-human. Is the force the first cause of nature, the *causa sua?* Imagine it as Kant's intelligible world, Hegel's absolute idea, Schopenhauer's will, Hartmann's unconscious will and intellect, Volkert's panlogism, Venetianer's panpsychism, or Mr. Tyndal's "unknowable," after all various constructions of the same substance; is it the first cause? Is it the unconditioned (*Das Unbedingte*) and conditioning (*Das Bedingende*), of which all objects of nature are the conditioned (*Das Bedingte*)? In case this question be answered in the affirmative, the next question is, what do we and can we know of God, nature, man, and their relations? How do we explain the progression of history, the duties of man, and the final cause of both? These, in my estimation, are the main questions of metaphysics, viz., the nature of the cause or causes which exist, figuratively spoken, behind physical nature, behind the mechanism of this cosmos and its parts, which are the effects thereof.

The term metaphysics in philosophy is of accidental origin. The first compiler of the writings of Aristotle found the works of that great master mind divided in logic, aesthetics, and physics, and placed last of all, hence behind physics Aristotle's principal work, and named it, therefore, metaphysics. Therefore, the province and limits of metaphysics have been variously understood by the philosophers. My definition is my own.

In metaphysics, the inductive method will not reach, to ascertain all reason is capable of ascertaining. Inasmuch as metaphysics undertakes to lift up the veil of nature, and to expose to intelligence that which is behind that veil as the cause of causes, the inductive method will do well; but where it begins to expound the nature of that cause, which is no sensual object; there are the limits of the law of causality, hence also of induction; there the province and methods of pure reason begin, and nothing else will solve that problem of problems. There are certainly more methods of cognition than philosophy expound and science applies. Knowledge precedes science, and cognition is prior to philosophy. Mankind knows vastly more than science and philosophy have utilized and systematized. The child sucking its nutriment performs mechanical feats, which only after thousands of years science began to construct. The entire material of philosophy in all its disciplines consists after all of the spontaneous productions of the mind. Philosophy discovered the form, it invented not the substance of its contents.

There is room left for genius to carve out new methods of cognition. Do I not know it *a priori?* I know that there is a God, a Providence, and an immortality, and I know it as sure as I know anything; yet I am not superstitious, ignorant, or credulous; I know all the methods of cognition and evidence in philosophy and science; still I may fail in convincing others of the correctness of my convictions, simply because the methods of cognition and evidence are not exhausted.

The most prominent and most profound metaphysicians in history are the Hebrews, not only those who wrote the Biblical Books, but also those who wrote the apocryphal, profane, and rabbinical works between 300 years before and 300 after the Christian Era, in Palestine and Egypt; and those of the Moorish-Spanish period from the tenth to the fifteenth centuries. They furnished the whole material, which metaphysicians have cast into the philosophical form, from Aristotle down to our days. Take away the Hebrew material from metaphysics, and what is left of it, is its formal portion, into which some indigestible dogmas are artificially pressed.

And now returning to our problem, we must discuss,

force once more. The forces co-operate in producing teleological centers. Whatever is a *causalnexus* is also a teleological center. Whatever object of nature we may examine represents a number of forces co-operating, co-ordinate, sub-ordinate or both. Take for instance any piece of common coal, and you have in it cohesion, attraction, gravitation, heat and light differentiated, hence also electricity and magnet. These forces are in the coal, immanent and permanent, insulated from the body of the universe, and bound together to constitute that particular object, that piece of coal.

How do those forces meet and how keep together to constitute that particular object? Only one of the three possibilities will explain the phenomenon: Either the forces bear in themselves, by affinity or attraction, the converging tendency and coherent nature; ·or all forces are actually but one, differently modified by chemical causes; or there is a superior and governing force, which unites and keeps bound together various inferior forces, to constitute and sustain intact any given object of nature. The convergence of forces is impossible, because they are variously connected in various limited objects, to the exclusion of any further connection with other forces or more force. If convergence was in the nature of all forces, they must unite indefinitely, so that there could be only one kind of objects with the same qualities precisely, and all matter must at last unite to one lump. Besides, death, decay, dissolution, or even the transition of qualities would be impossible on account of the constancy of force: so that the forces once united to an individual object must, by virtue of their convergence, remain forever intact; which we know not to be the case.

If we admit the unity or correlation of forces dematerialized, in their cosmic state, still this unity of forces exists not in their materialized state, in the objects of nature; for we can expel a force from a body, make it cosmic, and the other or others remain therein. You lay a piece of magnetized iron in the fire and expel the magnet, while other forces remain intact in the iron. You stamp a rock to dust and expel its cohesion, while the other forces remain in the material. By heat or electricity you reduce a solid to a liquid and a gas finally, and expel the force of gravitation. So nearly every force may be expelled, dematerialized and made cosmic, from any object of nature, without injury to others. Besides, if there was a unity of forces in matter, it could present but one kind of quality, which we know not to be the case.

Consequently only one possibility is left, viz., there is a superior and governing force which unites inferior forces in various relations and proportions, to form and to sustain intact the various objects of nature, each of which is a teleological center; and as soon as the influence of that superior force is withdrawn from any natural object, the remaining inferior forces, by their inherent tendency, strive to become again cosmic, which changes the respective bulk of matter in death, decay, dissolution, and would end with the reduction thereof to its elementary or cosmic state, if not arrested by that superior force. So, and not otherwise, life and death, differentiation and indifferentiation, being and dissolution, convergence and divergence in all forms can be understood. Therefore no object of nature can be duplicated by human ingenuity, simply because that superior and governing force is not, and most likely will never be, under man's control.

I beg you, ladies and gentlemen, to take particular notice of this point: The natural objects themselves, granite or tree, diamond or beast, metal or man, pebble or sun, forcibly and irresistibly suggest the necessary existence of a superior and governing force, by which each and all of them become, are, and return to, the cosmos. This superior and governing force is as evident to our mind as our self-consciousness, and as perceptible to our senses as the natural objects themselves are. What Aristotle called *morphe*, the form, that something which makes every particular object to what it actually is, with those peculiar qualities which it manifests, is the superior force which governs all others and modifies matter and inferior forces accordingly. This is no hypothesis, no theory; it is law, universal and undeniable.

I beg leave, ladies and gentlemen, to remind you that in biology we have discovered a similar superior and governing force of organic kingdoms, which was called there vital force. Then we have ascertained that vital force, life, will, and intellect are in fact one substance with these discernable attributes. Then we have ascertained in the teleology of history that the same force is also the Logos of History and Justice, commonly called Providence. Now we have established an analogous force, governing and superior, also in the inorganic kingdoms. Also here is will as the profuse variety of the objects of nature demonstrate; hence, also here is freedom. Also here is intellect, as the presence of will proves; and as every object of nature is in itself a teleological center, being co-ordinate and sub-ordinate to the cosmos, its law, order, and harmony. Also here is a genius of inorganic nature, which combines, proportions, shapes, and overrules inferior forces, to bring forth and to sustain these objects of nature and with them also the cosmos. Hence either these various superior and governing forces are identical, or we have arrived at the existence of several Gods, one of organic and another of inorganic nature, one of nature and another of history. I say "gods," although this word is still postulated only; but I will prove hereafter that the term is used in its proper signification.

Ancient nations understood this quite well, therefore their gods or genii for every class of natural objects, and their superior gods presiding over those inferior spirits, to account for the order and harmony in the cosmos. So the Kabbalistic Jews had their presiding angels, not only over the various elements and forces, but also over the special classes of natural objects, which play a considerable part in the philosophy of the Middle Ages. One of them was the *Sechel hap-poel*, the active or energetic reason, the Genius of Man and History, *Metathronos* who was Paul's pattern in shaping his Jesus.

It had been partly shown before, that the Logos of History manifests the same laws precisely as the Genius of Inorganic Nature; therefore we called history the continuation of the earth's creation. With man's appearance on earth, physical creation closed and mental creation began; the pedestal was finished and the statuary was placed upon it. Geology proves this abundantly.

As far back as science permits us to look, we can only think of matter in its primary elements, isolated, with no force acting upon it. Whether this matter in its zero state was in God, outside of Him, or created by Him, is a question of no particular importance to us; therefore I postulate, it was. Chemistry knows of elements only; atoms or molecules are creatures of science or imagination; elements only are thinkable or imaginable. These elements, however numerous, must have existed as parallels without convergence. No force being in them, there was neither affinity nor attraction. The first act of creation of this or any other solar system, this or any other planet, was the compression or concussion of these elements. This produced heat, and in such immense quantity, that the facit of its calculation sounds fabulous;

yet the collision of the elements must have produced an amount of heat corresponding to the mass and the force of concussion. Now all the elements, say of this earth, were one chaotic mass of burning liquid. With heat there came light, electricity, and motion, the unity of which is doubtful no longer. So first was the *Tohn Wabohu*, viz., the parallels of elementary matter in space. Then "God said let there be light and there was light," *i. e.*, there was heat, light, electricity, and motion, convertible into one another. Electricity, of course, must have been dynamical, now known as galvanic. Frictional and magnetic electricity could develop only after the mass had cooled off and metallic formations had ensued.

With the compression or concussion of the primary elements, the force of cohesion, chemical affinity, and molecular attraction was also imparted to the chaotic liquid, developing gradually, in which there was action and reaction in the form of contraction and expansion. Contraction may be the reaction of expansion by the mere contact of the fiery liquid with cold space; or expansion may be the reaction of contraction by the rarified and porous state of the heated liquid, and this may translate heat into light, electricity, and motion. At any rate only one force was originally imparted to the elements, by which the creation and formation of this earth was effected, and from which all the other forces were gradually developed. Therefore in our days the correlation of forces in their cosmic state is doubted no longer in science. All physical forces are a unit.

After a brief reflection, however, we discover that the force of compression must have preceded the force of expansion; for the very first act of creation was the compression or concussion of the elementary parallels. In fact, expansion became a force, after compression had united elementary matter and imbued it with force. It is in the nature of force to strive perpetually to become cosmic, to separate itself from the material objects, in which it is kept insolated by the superior and governing force. So it is in the nature of matter to dissolve into its primary elements, unless kept together by force, these two tendencies form the groundwork of the force of expansion, therefore before force and matter were united, and the parallels of matter were compressed to a body or bodies, there could be no force of expansion in them; hence compression is the original force. Here then we have precisely the same force at the bottom of creation which we have discovered as the superior and governing force in all objects of nature, viz., compression forming and preserving intact all objects of nature, of which all other physical forces are derivatives, consequently subject to its control. Also planetary attraction and repulsion are reactions of the force of compression, in fact all creations and preservation result from compression, but we can not enlarge here on this topic.

One force in this earth is, all others are reactions thereof; and this one force was originally the impulse imparted to the elementary parallels of matter, by the substance. And so we have arrived again at one substantial force, in the creation and preservation of all natural objects, or if this is identical with God, at the existence of one God. This first creative impulse is represented in the Bible, thus: "And the spirit of God moved upon the face of the waters"; not in the water, but upon its surface, because it was the force of compression; not God Himself moved upon the water, but His spirit, wind, *pneuma*, will, because it was an impulse imparted to the elementary parallels.

This first impulse could not have been the work of chance or casualty; for in all which comes within the cognition of man, in organic or inorganic nature, in history, or even in imagination, there is not one phenomenon without a cause. In fact, the human mind is incapable of thinking of a causeless effect. Causality is not a mere category of the human understanding; like space, it is a reality, inseparable from all which is, was, or will be. Hence the first impulse given to the elementary parallels must have proceeded from a cause, and all phenomena developing from that impulse to this moment must form one consecutive chain of cause and effect, although each object is a *causalnexus*.

An impulse is an action; an action is a function; and a function is in a substance only. Nothing can do nothing. Something only can do something. Hence the primary force which imparted the creative impulse to the elementary parallels is a substance, outside and above the earth and its forces, for which we have no better appellative than super-mundane.

There can be nothing in the effect which is not also in its cause. The cause in this case is super-mundane, consequently psychical; hence the forces themselves must be psychical, which in their action and reaction upon matter became materialized, and dematerialized again in their cosmic state. So we are enabled to form a clear conception of the origin of physical forces and their *quodity*.

We have now pressed the question onward to two psychical substances, one above inorganic nature and creation, and another above organic nature and history. We could well enough close here with the reasoning of Maimonides, Descartes, and Spinoza, that there can be only one psychical substance; or, calling this substance force, we could at once refer to the universality and unity of force; and we would have arrived already at the existence of one God. Still I have more evidence on hand, of which Maimonides, Descrates, and Spinoza made no use, and propose to produce it in my next lectures.

LECTURE XX.

ON METAPHYSICS—II. LECTURE, NATURE'S GOD.

LADIES AND GENTLEMEN.—I believe it may be set down as a general principle, wherever we have before us two or more effects, we have no right yet to postulate two substantial causes; for the difference of effect only points to a difference of functions, but by no means also to two substantial causes. Again the unity of the idea in any continuous chain of cause and effects excludes the possibility of two first causes. The material universe and the history of man are known to us as such a unity.

If these propositions are true, and I do not recollect that they have been doubted, then we need not prove the unity of the two postulated gods of our last lecture, viz., the Genius of the inorganic kingdom and creation, and the Logos of the organic kingdom and history. Any division of the first cause could be conceptional only, never real. Every dualism, trinitarianism or polytheism in the first cause is necessarily false.

In the special question before us, the analogy of the different phenomena points distinctly to the identity of the cause. The main force in the inorganic kingdom becomes phenomenal in the form of contraction and expansion. The contraction or compression, we have noticed as the continuous activity of the primary force, of the impulse imparted originally to inert matter. Expansion, is the inherent tendency of matter, to dissolve into its primary elements, to fall apart and become cosmic. This is not a force, but a negative thereof, a first, passive, and zero condition which produces no effect. All phenomenal effects are resultants of active forces, which are derivatives of the first impulse, the superior and governing force, known to us in the form of contraction or compression. This is self-evident to the chemist who reduces solid to liquid, liquid to gas and ether, by expelling the forces from matter, which he liberates and reduces to its primary, passive and zero state, as far as he can.

The same main force, however, becomes phenomenal also in organic nature, only that it developes new functions. It is attraction and repulsion, positive and negative electricity, north and south poles in the magnet, centrifugal and centripetal power, or however it becomes phenomenal. We observe the same fundamental action in the cell or even protoplasm, contraction and expansion, and by it accretion and secretion, internal motion and external limitation. This is the fundamental function of all organic life. Then it re-appears in animal instinct, in man's selfishness and social nature, as well as his struggle for personal freedom and patriotism, to be at the same time an independent individual and a dependent citizen of a large, populous, and powerful community, which is the primary cause of all history, with its two similar elements of conservatism and progressionism. It is always the same fundamental principle of contraction and expansion, only that a variety of new functions of the same cause become phenomenal under new circumstances. Hence, we have not the least ground for the supposition of two first causes.

Nor, indeed, is there any reason to think of another first cause somewhere outside of this solar system, as we know the same force and matter to be universal. If there is anything certain in the teachings of astronomy, it is beyond a doubt, that light, motion and attraction appertain to all celestial bodies. These forces being derivatives of the first impulse, the superior and governing force, hence the same first cause everywhere; although in the materialization of force, other derivatives may be active on other stars, and produce modifications of matter unknown to us.

Again, by the spectrum analysis and by the meteors or aerolites reaching our earth from different regions, we know that matter is matter everywhere, of the same substance and qualities, although elements, in consequence of other derivative forces, may combine to different compositions in different stars. The possibility of combinations of one hundred elements, and there are certainly rather more than less, is almost infinite; but every combination remains the same matter subject to the same force. So all possible varieties and modifications of matter would not point to a second original cause. Therefore, there can be little doubt, that all celestial bodies, however different their atmospheres, rotations, and relations to this or any other sun, are populated with living beings, in correspondence with those various conditions; and there like here, the last link in the chain must be intelligent beings akin to man.

But aside of all these considerations, the unity of the first cause is proved by the teleology of creation, being, and history. Every stage of the earth's formation, every individual object of nature, and every period of man's history, as we have noticed before, is a teleological center, the end, aim, and object of a design and purpose, a logical sequence of prior causes, back to the first cause. In every stage of the earth's formation and every period of history, as in every individual object of nature, as a necessary part of the cosmos, there is again the germ and efficient cause to the next following ones, and so on from the first impulse imparted to the elementary parallels, to the present stage of the earth and period of history, So and not otherwise we can understand the continuous chain of cause and effects phenomenal in every *causalnexus*, necessarily connected with the law of causality.

Therefore we are entitled at every point not only to the question of efficient causes, but also to the queries why and whereto, at every pause. Naturalists will never arrive at a proper understanding of nature, unless they search after the why and whereto at every stage of creation, and history, the objects of nature and their respective parts. The fact is, while one ascertains the efficient causes of one stage or period, he exposes the final causes of the prior stages or periods. Whatever is efficient cause in any higher stage, was final cause in the lower one. This is the unmistakable architecture of nature and history. Science may not succeed in this or the next century to ascertain in all instances all efficient and final causes; but it will certainly solve one problem after the other, and unless they are infinite, they must certainly be solved one day or another. When the law of nature and history will be scientifically established we will be enabled to see the final causes, without being prophets, and then the final causes must unravel to us the mystery of the final cause. Nothing is unknowable.

When the first impulse was imparted to the elementary parallels to unite and mingle by compression or concussion, this impulse was the efficient cause; the final cause was the unification of the elements and the ensuing heat of about 2,000 degrees F., taking the medium number between the extremes; and this was stage No. 1. The liquid and radiating fire ball which, from the proper distance. must have looked like a sun, was stage No. 2, to which stage No. 1 contained the efficient cause, and of which it was the final cause. But this fire ball was not to remain in *statu-quo*. By the forces evolving from the first impulse and materializing in the fiery liquid, it moved around its axis and in some orbit around the sun. Gradually it cooled off, formed a solid nucleus and crust, the radiating heat carring off the various gases, formed an atmosphere, thick, heavy and pregnant also with the elements which afterwards formed the outer crust of the earth, and the ocean. When the surface of the young earth was cooled down to about 200 degrees F. the gases attracted from the atmosphere covered the earth, all, or nearly so, with water of a peculiar thickness; and yet there was a division, an expansion, a firmament, between the water on the earth and that above it still suspended in the thick and heavy atmosphere, through which the rays of the sun light penetrated sparingly. It was stage No. 3, the earth was in a condition to bring forth organic beings; and this stage No. 3, was the final cause of stages No. 1 and 2, which contained its efficient causes.

Was this stage creation's objective point? Certainly not. If it had been it must have stopped there, which it did not. New functions of the first cause become now phenomenal, organic beings of the lowest forms are brought forth in the thick and hot water, the lowest forms of vegetables and animals, rising gradually in the scale of evolution to huge monsters. Here the final cause of all former stages becomes phenomenal in the existence of living beings. The first impulse imparted to matter by its materialized derivatives has overcome the primary tendency of matter to dissolve and separate in its elements; there is an earth of one piece, covered with a continuous sheet of water—and attempts now to come forth from its unconscious to the conscious condition in animal centers, to which the vegetables are the state of transition in the gradual evolution and differentiation. Here then we have stage No. 4, the start of conscious centers, in which the force captivated in matter attempts its liberation, after it had overcome inert matter to that extent that organic formation had become possible; and here again stage No. 4 is the final cause of stages Nos. 1, 2, and 3 which contain its efficient causes.

Following up the progress of creation, we observe how the formation of the earth's crust, the change of atmosphere, and the development of vegetable and animal life go hand in hand in the regular routine of cause and effect. As the water is distilling, its sediments settle down to the bottom, the fish make their appearance. As the water recedes and swamps ensue, the amphibies follow, always preceded by their food. As the earth attracts the carbon from the atmosphere, producing huge vegetation, the birds, carbon inhaling, come in existence, food and shelter preceded them. And when the carbon enveloping the earth like a thick cloud had been sufficiently attracted by the earth, sun, moon and stars become visible on the earth. Here we have stage No. 5, the earth covered with rich vegetation, land and ocean populated with radiates, mollusks, and articulates of most beauteous forms, together with fishes, amphibies, and birds, now under the direct influence of the sun and the other celestial bodies, and the earth in its proper orbit. The obscure gloom has passed away and the age of light has commenced on earth. The primary force materialized in the earth is reunited with the cosmic light, has liberated itself from the state of gloomy obscurity. Here is stage No. 5, the final cause of stages No. 1, 2, 3, 4, with its efficient causes in all of them.

Now come the creatures of light, the constant types. Now, and not before, the mammals could make their appearance. Elementary matter had first to be brought so far under the control of the active force before it could achieve its liberation from the material bonds of unconsciousness. But it progresses rapidly through all transitory forms of the vegetable and animal kingdoms, through all phases of conscious beings, always imparting to matter higher morphic qualities, preparing it for higher formations, until the last triumph is achieved, viz., the unconscious has become conscious in the animal kingdom, with the vegetables as its points of transition; now the conscious becomes self-conscious in man, with the animals as points of transition. The primary force becomes self-conscious itself again, in the self-conscious man, who, knowing all in his consciousness, distinguishes himself from all; and this is his self-consciousness. The first cause has become itself again, the self-conscious psychical cause of all forces and all motion in matter. So the ring of creation was completed with stage No. 6, with its efficient causes in stages 1, 2, 3, 4, and 5, of all of which it is the final cause and teleological center.

But here the work is not finished, for man is not fully self-conscious until he knows all which is knowable, to distinguish himself from all which is, and consequently the work of this cause is not completed with the earth's and other planets' creation. Here begins stage No. 7, man's history. It is the Creator's Sabbath. The work of liberation from matter and the triumph over it, begins in man, by him, and for him. He works on to accomplish the subjugation of matter, the resurrection of self-conscious spirit, the triumph of life over death, of light over darkness, of self-conscious intelligence over blind and inexorable powers of darkness; of freedom, love, and happiness over cold and barren necessity. This is the creation of history, the progress of the primary force to self-conscious existence in the human family, and the stages thereof are well marked in the works of intelligent historians. Therefore the Bible states: "And on the seventh day (not on the sixth) God completed His work which He had made; and He ceased to work on the seventh day from all the work He had made (for here man's work begins). And God blessed the seventh day and sanctified it, because then He had ceased from all His work, which God had created to do" (to go on and on to perfection with the progression of man's history). This stage, No. 7, is the final cause of all previous stages which contain its efficient causes.

You see, ladies and gentlemen, it is all one piece, of one cast, one chain of cause and effects, one design, one object, all of which must have been present in stage No. 1 and in each succeeding stage. All of them were in the first, the last in the first, and all in each, which the ancient Hebrews described as:

סוף מעשה במחשבה תחלה

"The end of the work contained in the first thought."

Here then is one will, intellect, and design, one object and one executive power, one spirit, one piece of inevitable logic, from which no iota can be taken away, none added, and none inverted. Here the bare possibility of more than one first cause falls to the ground. As soon as intelligence claims its right to look upon the cosmos through the law of causality, it is led forward and backward through the unbroken chain to the final cause and to the first cause, which reveals its nature in its own last triumphs, in the self-conscious intelligence of man.

He, the substance, who has imparted this first impulse to the parallels of matter, of this and any other planet or solar system, the impulse from which all forces of nature have ensued, and by evolution and differentiation, constructed this great cosmos, triumphs over all matter in the self-conscious intelligence of man, remains in him and over him, preserving and governing all, shaping all destinies, guiding all and constantly from lower to higher conditions; He who is the Genius of nature and the Logos of history, fills all space and is the force of all forces; He is the Cosmic God, for He is the cause of all causes, the first principle of all things, the only substance whose attributes are life, will, and intellect. Matter is the non-substance, for it has no functions; it is the inert, passive, and imperceptible material, which He, by the forces, moves, shapes, subjects, and governs. He is Almighty, for He is the force of all forces, the cause of all causes. He is omnipresent, revealed everywhere by the ever-active force of all forces in nature, and every motion of the human intellect. He is omniprescent, for He fills all space and penetrates all atomic matter. He is all-wise and omniscient, for He is the intellect of all intellect, its cause and substance. He is the Preserver and Governor, for He is the will, freedom, and justice. He is the Cosmic God, who is not anthropomorphous. He is not in heaven above nor on earth below, for He is everywhere, in all space, in all objects of nature, in every attribute of matter, and in every thought of the mind. "No man can see me and live." He appeared to none, because He continually and simultaneously appears to all and through all. He spoke to none, because He speaks eternally and simultaneously to all and through all. He resides nowhere especially, because He is everywhere continually. He had no beginning, because He made it; and no end, because He has no beginning. He changes not, because all changes are effects, and He is the cause of all causes and no effect. He is the Cosmic God,—the only God,—whose name is ineffable, who alone is, was, and will be forever and aye, whose existence none can deny, and whose immensity none can comprehend. We know, we feel His immeasureable grandeur, and worship Him with awe.

Scientists, here is your God and Lord, whom you seek, and whom to find is the highest wisdom. He is the God found by induction and felt by spontaneity. Philosophers, here is your God, whom to expound is the highest glory of human mind—Kant, and other thinkers, have argued against the anthropomorphous God of theology; the cosmic God is philosophy's first and last substance. Simple-minded men, here is your God, whom you need not seek, for He is everywhere, in you and about you, in every quality of matter and every motion of the mind; where you are, He is; where you observe or think, you think Him. Children, here is your God, in the fragrance of your flowers, in the beauteous hues of vernal blossoms, in the thunder and the whisper, in heaven's azure dome and earth's verdant garb, in your innocent smiles and your mother's sweet tenderness. Sage or fool, great or little, here is your God, you can not escape Him, and He cannot escape you; He is in you, and you are in Him. Men of all future generations, here is God in the harmony of all human conceptions and knowledge, the God of all, and all eternity, the Cosmic God, the GREAT I AM, and none beside Him.

Thanks to the Almighty, that He has permitted us to look into the mysteries of His creation; that He has led and guided us through the obscure regions of this material world, onward, forward, heavenward, always on the simple path of induction, to His very throne, to simple, sublime, and eternal truth for all coming generations. Humbly and gratefully I render praise and thanksgiving to the Eternal who has permitted me to conceive these thoughts, combinations, and conclusions, which have led me back home to the one and eternal God. My soul triumphs before Him at this immortal victory.

So far, in this particular point, induction leads. Here deduction begins, and here ends our province at present. But we have three more problems to solve, viz., What is nature? What is man? Which is the relation of God, nature, and man? I propose to begin the discussion of these problems in my next lecture.

LECTURE XXI.

NATURE AND ITS RELATION TO DEITY.

LADIES AND GENTLEMEN.—Nature like nature's God is a word much abused, often uttered and seldom understood. Among a thousand probably who use this word, there is no more than one who thinks of nature's magnitude, vastness, grandeur, and intricate mechanism, surpassing thought and bewildering contemplation; and among a million using this term, there is sometimes scarcely one who has formed a clear idea of it. When you hear the atheist or gross materialist declaim of dame nature as a personified mother, or utter expressions like this: "Every thing is natural, it is all by and in nature, nature is the mother of all things, nature does all," and similar expressions, you hear just as many empty and unmeaning words, of which fact you can convince yourselves in a moment, by asking the simple question, What is nature? and the answer received will be as shallow and uncertain as the declamations you had been treated to.

It appears to me: Nature is the combination of force and matter, and the causal activity of the former in the latter in this substance and all its phenomenal modifications. The derivation of the term from *natus* and *nasci* "to be born," points to continual birth, as it were, of phenomenal modifications, and to a substantial cause behind the phenomena, by which birth is given.

Nature, therefore, contains four distinct ideas: The forces which manifest themselves and the matter in which it is manifested, which in their union form created substance; the causation in this substance and the *modus operandi*, or causality and modality; and the individual objects of nature, continually rising and falling in the created substance, or individuation—all of which is contained in the four categories: Substantial existence, causation, modality and phenomenal being, which are the foundation of all existence, and also of the ten categories of Aristotle.

Whatever being or attribute of a being springs from those four cardinal ideas is to be called natural. Secondary significations of the terms nature or natural do not concern us here.

When we say the world or the universe, we usually mean, in the abstract, nature at rest, *i. e.* space and its contents without reference to motion, activity, or causation. When we say cosmos, we mean, again in the abstract, nature at work, in reference to its law, order and harmony, and without reference to its substance or material. Both world and cosmos are contained in the term nature.

We have said nothing about time, because it is a nonentity; it is a category of *a priori* thought in reference of planetary revolution. Eternity means no time. We compute time, not on account of its reality but on account of our perishable nature and the revolution of the planets. Time must be deduced from nature and placed within the sphere of human reason. In our dreams time disappears; so it does with the somnambulist, and wherever self-consciousness is suspended. Animals have as little an idea of time, as they have of numbers. We arrive at the idea of time by our pulsations and the planetary motions. What we on this earth call time and the beginning of time, the *Bereshith*, as reads the first word of the Bible, could begin with the rotation of this earth only. On other planets, time had another beginning, and consists of other divisions; and wherever there are no self-conscious beings, there is no time.

Space is the continuity of the substance. All is in space and nothing outside thereof. There is no outside thereof. Space is the reality itself. It is not merely the Where? of all realities, also not a mere category of *a priori* thought; it is the substance, the force, the first cause, God's habitation, and infinite extension, in fact indivisible, is an attribute of the substance. There is another time but the same space on every planet.

There is but one substance, and this one is psychical. This one psychical substance with the knowable attributes of life, will, intellect and extension is spirit, the Cosmic God. Matter whether in the Deity or of the Deity, neither of which can be positively denied or affirmed by experience and induction, is no substance; because without the influence of force, in its primary and elementary state it has no attributes and no qualities, no activity and no influence; it is the passive and indifferent zero. Whatever is, must demonstrate existence of itself; primary matter, by itself, is incapable of such demonstration, it is moved, formed and shaped, or made morphic, by force or forces, As functions proceed from a substance, so a substance must exercise functions. Hence matter is no substance.

It must be added here, that the eternity of matter was maintained in philosophy by Aristotle, and the whole perapatetic school. Among the Hebrews Ibn Gabirol and Gersonides defended this doctrine. Ibn Ezra thinks *bara*, the second word of the Bible, does not signify creation out of nothing. Maimonides thinks the arguments on both sides balance one another, and creation out of nothing is no indispensible Jewish dogma.

Wherever the force of the substance acts upon the elementary parallels of matter, the material substance is the resultant, in which all causes of the processes and developments of the created substance are immanent. With this combination of force and matter nature begins. It begins with the material substance in every solar system, and every planet with the beginning thereof. Therefore nature as it is now, was not created simultaneously; nor do experience and induction entitle us, to fix any time for the creation of this or any other planet or solar system, or even for the formation of any of the earth's strata under the entire different conditions of heat, motion, electricity and magnet, the æriform, vaporous or liquid state of the material.

All causes for the processes and developments of the material substance being immanent therein, it is also the beginning of the law of causality on each planet; *i. e.* the processes and developments follow in the regular routine of cause and effect, of which one of the Psalm poets said חוק נתן ולא יעבר "He hath given a law and he will not trespass it." The derivative forces materialized in nature, work on and on, as the supreme intellect has originally designed it producing at every onward step teleological centers, which contain the final cause of previous conditions, hence each is a *causalnexus*, and bears in itself the efficient cause for the next following teleological center. All that is, is by the causal activity of force in matter. It is nature's second step.

Inasmuch, however, as all solar systems and planets consist of the same material substance, the same force and matter and the same routine of cause and effect; furthermore, inasmuch as all forces are derivatives and materializations of the one primary and central force; there is substantial affinity among all planetary bodies, mediated by the central force, in the forms of attraction and repulsion. So the whole material world is a unit, a cosmos and no chaos, in the regular routine of cause and effect, one grand organism, pervaded by the vital force in the unconscious state, so that each part, however minute or immense, must perform intelligently its functions in co-ordination and sub-ordination with all other parts, as is the case in every organic body. That the law of causality extends all over the material world, is sufficiently demonstrated by the calculations and predictions of astronomy, and the laws governing that science. Next we must take into consideration the problem, if all planets were not created simultaneously, and that they were not is generally admitted, how could the existing ones keep in their orbits without the attraction of their neighboring planets not yet in existence? The same question is legitimate in regard to solar systems. Here plain facts compel us, in planetary attraction; to affirm the manifestation of the central, primary, superior and governing force, which regulates substantial affinity, attraction and repulsion. Space is not filled with forces, it is force itself, from which the various forms of force in matter issue. It consists not of atomic and impenetrable matter; it is psychical, it is substance, and there is neither atom nor impenetrability, as little as either is in feeling, consciousness or thought. Therefore the motion of planetary bodies is regulated by the primary force, in the Cosmic God, before the existence of the planetary neighbors, whose attraction then regulates motion.

But here the atheist or gross materialist steps in and maintains, it is all by the laws of nature; *i. e.*, the laws of nature are personified into the superior and governing force with intellect and will, as though without either they could not govern the material universe in order and harmony. The supposed laws of nature are metamorphozed into as many gods. I admit the existence of nature, and deny the existence of laws therein as an active principle. What are the laws of nature? The constant repetition of the same phenomena or effects from the same cause or causes, is called a law of nature. You see, the laws of nature are "constant repetitions," and are no more substantial that the laws of a state or city. They express in general principle the modality, the *modus operandi* of force ; consequently they are formal only, expressing the relations of the thinking mind to the different modes of being, as classified under the ten categories, or probably under my four. Therefore the laws of nature are abstractions of the human mind, are in the same and not in material nature, where force is the perpetual originator of cause and effect. The laws as such, if anywhere outside of the human mind, can be in the divine mind only. There, I will add, there they must be. For the forces are the cause of the regular succession of cause and effect in undisturbed harmony; and all forces are materialized derivatives of the primary force which is a function of the substance, hence of God. There can be nothing in the effect which is not also in the cause; hence the whole chain of cause and effect, all the processes and developments of the material substance, the whole system of evolution and differentiation to the very end of existence, must have been present in the substance prior to the first act of creation, and must have been imparted to the material substance with the very first impulse, or else causation was not immanent in nature. This is the omniscience of the Cosmic God, He being the cause of all causes inclusive of all possible effects, as each effect in its turn becomes cause again. All laws of nature being formal abstractions of the perpetual continuity of cause and effect, must be present in the divine mind.

Here is reality of the universal spirit, fictitiously postulated by La Place. Dubois admits the probable reality of this universal spirit; but he says, I can find no brain in the universe, and brain according to that physiologist and others is the cause of thought, consciousness, reason, etc., *i. e.*, the machine generates its own force, not only by which it works, but also by which it has become a machine. This, however, is no objection to us who know the presence of will and intellect in every manifestation of force, crystal or blade of grass, bud or blossom, polyp or man, cell or sun. This is certainly no objection with us, who hold there can be no effect without an adequate cause, and there can be nothing in the effect which is not also in the cause ; hence all organisms and every part thereof, all as a unit, parts of which are actualized in the various plants and animals, must be first in the organizing force, in the vital force, in the primary force, in the substance. Every morphic idea actualized anywhere must be in the primary force, in the substance of which it is a function, and all morphic ideas must be a unit in the one and universal force. Hence God is the organism of all organisms, if Mr. Dubois wants it expressed so, not merely potential but actual, for what we call actual in matter is really actual in the universal mind and potential in matter as its moving cause. We, of course, would express it so: The cause contains more than the aggregate of its effects, anyhow it must contain each of its effects. Will and intellect, appearing as effects, in the individuals from a cause in the substance, must be infinitely greater in the cause than in all effects thereof. So Mr. Dubois might find also a brain in the grand organism of nature, which is not necessary for us, to whom brain is not the cause but an effect of will and intellect and their momentary apparatus.

Here, however, Hegel and the Heglians, down to Ludwig Noire, Schoppenhauer, Ed. von Hartmann, Volkert, Venetianer, Huxley, Spencer, and a few more, besides David Frederic Strauss, chime in: Provided the Cosmic God is self-conscious, the laws of nature are present in his consciousness; if not, not. Not having discussed yet the question of consciousness and self-consciousness in general, I can not apply them here understandingly, and must postpone this question till my next lecture. Still, on the strength of the foregoing argument, I am entitled to postulate, that intellect materialized becomes unconscious; intellect itself dematerialized is always self-conscious. The forces of nature are psychical and substantial, but they are materialized; hence intellect in the inorganic matter is unconscious will, therefore it is always logical and always reaches its aims and purposes. When we speak of natural forces, we actually speak of as many ideas in the divine mind. The ideas themselves are unconscious, but they are always in a self-conscious mind, as is the case with all ideas of which we have any cognition. So God is immanent in nature, omnipresent therein as the cause thereof, and revealed in every phenomenon, and in every quality of matter, by active force. It must always be borne in mind that in the substance thought means deed, an ideal fact; thinking is real in connection with omnipotence. When you have an idea, you may have a volition to do so, and consider whether you should and could or not; all of which is not the case in the Deity.

Again as this material nature is only a small fraction of the universe, the worlds are mere points in space; God is not inhumated, interred, incarnated, or materialized in nature. The cause is not lost in its effects, not submerged and not exhausted in them. The cause remains the cause forever, independent of all effects, and infinitely more than the aggregate of its effects. God is inceptive in the mathematical sense of this term. He is the universe, and material nature is in Him; but he is not exhausted therein. The Cosmic God is not outside of the universe, nothing can be thought or imagined outside thereof, but He is outside of material nature as well as inside thereof; therefore we call Him the super-mundane God.

The natural forces being psychical and unconscious in their materialized state, seek liberation from unconsciousness, and break through the material bonds in the organic kingdoms, in the centers of consciousness and self-consciousness, and so the primary force becomes gradually itself again in uncounted millions of ideas.

Here is one of our great advantages over materialism. It can not account for consciousness, the simplest sensation or feeling, or even the formation of a cell or a protoplasm. Where the infusorium with its red point of eyes sees rays of light, or the polypees the living infusorium, where a sea-weed or a blade of grass grows, or a spider weaves its web, the philosophy of materialism is at an end, simply because its premises are erroneous and false. We know the tree by its fruits. With us, however, the whole process of nature is a unit. The primary force is vital force, is will and intellect, consequently all causes of organic life and functions are in it. It overcomes and metamorphozes matter gradually and systematically prepares organic buds on the tree of life, unfolds them to blossoms of consciousness, and ripens them to fruits of self-consciousness. Conscious centers are produced by the same force which created the material substance, preserves and governs it, and individuates itself therein. It is the psychical force becoming itself again. It is its victory over matter.

With us also many absurd questions fall to the ground. What does God do, if the forces of nature do it all?—is one of those absurd queries. Where are the derivative forces, if their efficient cause be withdrawn? we ask in return, and the only reply is, if God should withdraw himself from nature, it would become again *Tohu Ubohu*. The cause removed and the effects are no more. Why did God not create this world or others millions of years before? is another absurdity with us, who know that time is a nonentity, and the nonentity can not be taken into consideration. Who made God? is probably the most absurd of all absurd questions. God is the First Cause, and an endless regression of causes is in itself absurd, as Aristotle already discovered.

With us there is only one God, one substance, and this is psychical. He is the universe, and the force; life, freedom, will, intellect, are his cardinal attributes, which include omnipotence, omniscience, omnipresence, and supreme justice. Matter without force is the non-substance, the indifferent zero. Nature is the created substance of force and matter, and is continually in God and under his control. The natural forces are materialized derivaties from the primary force, which is a function of the substance, and like it psychical. In 'the organic beings the primary force becomes again itself, conscious and then self-conscious in man. The creation and nature of man is no less plain and simple in this unity of architecture; but we must postpone this subject to our next lecture.

LECTURE XXII.

MAN IN HIS RELATIONS TO GOD AND NATURE.

LADIES AND GENTLEMEN.—Nature's beauty, grandeur, and sublimity, exist in the aesthetical consciousness of intelligent beings; hence on earth in man only. The mind is not merely the mirror of nature, it is nature's magic wand which enlivens the reflexes and adorns them with the charms and graces which it possesses. In man, nature or the first cause of this planet, becomes self-conscious, itself again. Imagination is the kaleidescope turned by the senses and phantasy. Consciousness is the mind's animating and animated focus, where nature collects and recognizes itself again. In its highest degree, consciousness is the utmost, the *ne plus ultra* of nature, in which the whole cycle of evolutions is completed. The self-conscious cause of this planet's creation, has become self-conscious, itself again.

Therefore consciousness is nature's final cause, its last object and highest function. It must be admitted, either this cosmos has no object of existence, or it exists to be known, admired, and enjoyed, which makes the existence of conscious beings necessary as the final cause. We know that nature is the work of intelligence; and intelligence, such is the law of its nature, is always at work to accomplish preconcerted ends. In the common transactions of our every-day life, we expect everywhere a premeditated end of intelligent labor, simply because it is the law of intelligence. Let us add here, that it is certainly absurd to expect more wisdom of the differentiated than of the universal intellect. Therefore nature has a final cause which must have been premeditated in a self-consciousness and end again in self-consciousness, as nothing can come out of nothing, and no effect can be more than its cause.

Consciousness is of different degrees between infusorium and man. It comprises two elements, viz.: the objects outside, and the ideas inside of the conscious being, knowledge and being, so that it is both objective and subjective. It is the only organ which unites and harmonizes these two elements, so that it announces itself as the last ring in the chain of being, closing the circle of existence between the differentiated and universal intelligence, nature's final cause, the re-appearance of its first cause.

The different degrees of consciousness depend on its quality of intensity. Let us compare it, for illustration, to a light in the center of a conscious being, to be also its focus. The light of the lowest quality or intensity will diffuse its rays to but a short distance and illuminate but a few objects; hence few will be reflected in the focus. The light of the highest quality and intensity will reach and illuminate a large circle of objects, hence reflect many in its focus, and reflect them so much clearer and more distinct. Imagine a large plain, the horizon bounded by a chain of mountains here, a forest there, a lake yonder, with a variety of objects on it, all seen distinctly in the light of the sun. Then see the same plain in moon light; how much smaller, how many objects change their forms or disappear altogether; in a dark night with a torch light or a lantern in hand, you see less and less, and the objects seen become less distinct. So consciousness differs in various organic beings from infusorium to man up to great and comprehensive minds.

In the highest classes of animals, consciousness reaches not beyond the periphery of self-preservation, the individual, and the race. It becomes conscious of the objects which have some direct relation to its self-preservation, without the idea of number, time, cause, effect, color or shape. It is a kind of dim consciousness, called so because we have no word to express it correctly. The consciousness of man is of an entirely different quality. He sees the universe, or rather enough of it to form an idea of the whole; and in the universe he is conscious of forces, laws, mind, and God. He penetrates far beyond the periphery of self-preservation, and the objects within that line. He lifts the veil of sensual objects to recognize causes and the cause of causes. Man only knows nature, hence he alone can be nature's final cause, in whom the first cause becomes itself again.

The reflection of nature, metamorphozed to living ideas in man's consciousness, is so powerful in the focus, that man becomes the index of nature, a minature universe, in which he sees also himself and his own apparatus of cognition. He makes himself subject and object of his consciousness, the thinker, the thinking, and the object thought, *i. e.*, he is self-conscious. He recognizes himself with all his capacities and abilities, and the universe reflected in him. He recognizes the causes in him and outside of him, his own reality and universality together with the reality and universality outside of him, and the laws governing both. The cause of self-consciousness is certainly the intensity of consciousness, recognizing so many objects, causes, laws and effects which he must compare among themselves and to himself, that by the very law of contradiction, he must become self-conscious. Therefore animals can not be self-conscious, and among men it varies in degree according to the quantity and quality of cognitions and comparisons, so that the most powerful intellect, the most enlarged and enriched intelligence, the most active and exact mind developes the most powerful self-consciousness, in whom nature has become itself again.

Here we have arrived at another very important point, a prominent trait of human nature. Self-consciousness comprises not only all the mental functions of man, but also his moral character. Self-conscious beings only can be moral, for they and they only, know that the moral law, the *categoric imperative*, is the law of their own nature. To be moral signifies to obey the moral law as it is, and because it is a component part, a constituent of human nature. Morality from any other motive is far from perfection. There may be, and I have no doubt there are moral traits in all living beings, as Mr. Darwin and other biologists maintain, since the nature of the first cause is universally the same; there may be, and I have no doubt there are, moral traits in all human beings, however degraded or savage; but morality in the proper sense of the term depends on self-consciousness. One can be moral knowingly and wittingly only, that he obeys the laws of his own nature as a free agent. Therefore the various degrees of self-consciousness make also the various degrees of morality, so that with the loftiest self-consciousness only, the highest degree of morality is possible. Here is the philosophical foundation of ethics, but we cannot discuss it here, and will only add that the loftiest self-consciousness is in God, therefore also the perfection of morality.

Where is the cause of all that? Where and how do

consciousness, self-consciousness, and moral conscience awake in the living being, and what is the nature of that anomaly? They are not in the materialist's matter, in atoms, and atomic forces; hence the materialist replies, I do not know. They are not in Schopenhauer's irrational will as the world's substance, therefore he gives us no answer how the irrational becomes rational. They are not in Hartmann's unconscious will and intellect as the world's substance, hence here the very weakest point of that philosophy, as Volkert well remarks. Nor are they in Hegel's absolute idea, which, though logical, is no less unconscious and void of moral principle than Hartmann's unconscious substance; and all the pointed words used as to the self-division of the idea and the opposition of its parts, are void of any substantial meaning, as they name not the quodity of consciousness and morality. That these functions exist can as little be doubted as we can change the truisms, nothing can come from nothing, something only can produce something, and the effect must be in the cause. Hence we are compelled to place the cause back into the very nature of intellect, as an attribute thereof, and say intellect is always self-conscious and moral; therefore the first cause of this and every other planet must be self-conscious and moral. But we know that inorganic nature is neither, that the degrees vary in the organic beings as we descend the scale of organism to arrive finally at stupor and unconsciousness. We know that in all these phenomena we have but one first cause before us. Hence, the conclusion appears to me as irresistible as the *cogito ergo sum*, hence the first cause is self-conscious and moral; its derivative forces are unconscious in their materialization in nature, to break through matter, and by the gradual process of evolution make it fit of becoming organisms for self-conscious manifestations of intelligence; and in them the first cause becomes itself again in the differentiated state which is its victory over matter, while all the time the conscious and unconscious, the moral and immoral, are present in the self-consciousness and morality of the first cause which is God for ever.

This explains all phenomena, accidental or substantial, from the principle. So the vegetable kingdom is the transition from the unconscious to the conscious in matter; and the animal is the transition from the conscious to the self-conscious in man, with all gradations in both cases; and the natural man is the transition from the lowest to the highest degree of self-consciousness and morality in the man of culture and civilization, the man of history. It is all one first cause, developing gradually its various functions in the progression of evolutions. It is all self-conscious in the first cause to become again self-conscious in man. It is the fundamental principle of vital monism. It is also the philosophical foundation of moral theology, without ignoring one fact of science.

This refutes Emanuel Kant's supposition that we can not know the thing *per se* (das Ding an sich). We do know it as soon as we are sufficiently self-conscious. Man is the thing *per se*, matter and force, cause and effect, inorganic matter, solid, liquid, gas, vegetable, animal, spirit, unconscious, conscious, and self-conscious. He is nature's complete index, the mycrocosm in the macrocosm. He is matter's last gradation and the spirit's final triumph over it. Whenever man will have knowledge enough of himself and nature, he will easily discover in himself *das Ding an sich*.

So man's relation to God and nature is clear. He is the connecting link between both. He represents unconscious nature and self-conscious God. He stands under the control of nature's forces which he controls by the last triumph of mind over matter. He is continually the governor and the governed, the perpetual struggle and triumph of mind over matter, always progressing in the dominion of the conscious over the unconscious in the process of history. This leads us into the realm of history.

In countless millions of ideas, not one exactly like the other, the first cause of this planet has become conscious again; and in another unknown number of ideas it has become self-conscious, itself again, in human beings, differentiated and individualized with freedom. While the analogous traits of intellect under all circumstances point to one univeral intellect, the variety of capacities, abilities, talents, geniuses, and inclinations, point just as distinctly to freedom, individuality, personality, self-acting intellect and will in man. As such, to use a rabbinical metaphor, man is an associate of the Deity in the continuation of the creation. It is by the continuous development of human nature in the process of history to a higher degree of self-consciousness, that the first cause becomes more and more itself in man's triumphs over unconscious nature. So the progression of history is the progression of the first cause to its highest triumphs.

Man's self-consciousness increases with the increase of his knowledge, and with it, his moral nature grows in beautiful proportion and harmony. I do not mean to maintain that those who possess the most extensive learning are necessarily the most moral men, although as a general thing they are; I only maintain that self-consciousness is the cause, and morals the effect, and the effect can never be higher than its cause. With every onward step in knowledge and morality, man gains dominion over the lower realms of nature, the conscious subjugates the unconscious, and so he assists the Deity in the government of matter, the triumph of self conscious and moral intelligence. The history of philosophy marks the onward steps of growing self-consciousness; the history of government and religion marks out the onward march of morality, and the history of arts and inventions tells man's progress in the government of mechanical nature. The highest law for man is to advance himself and others in self-consciousness, morality, and dominion over mechanical nature, the triumph and mastery of the conscious over the unconscious, of mind over matter. So man fulfills his destiny in society, and elevates himself to an immortal personality. Here is the fundamental idea in philosophy for the doctrine of the soul's immortality.

History is the functional development of the first cause of this planet in the various personalities, each of whom is a self-conscious idea in that first cause, hence in God. Each period in history is the final cause of all preceding ones, and the last will be the final cause of all the former. Every person makes history as far as he fulfills his destiny. Each period of history is made by the persons acting at that period; hence every person fulfilling his destiny in history is in himself a final cause of creation and history.

Again as man's self consciousness grows with the increase of his knowledge, and his morality with his self-consciousness, he must necessarily live and co-operate with the society of progressive culture and civilization. For man receives most of his knowledge from man and the established institutions, least from his own observation and experience, and moral perfection can be reached in society only. Society and not the brain or nerves of the individual is the depository of actualized mind from all past ages, preserved in books, documents, works of art, articles of daily use, state and social organizations and establishments, customs, maxims, popularized principles, laws, moral and intellectual habits, modes of living, scholastic and educational establishments, and means of communication, multiplying and improving with every passing day.

The principle underlying the social problem is the perpetual re-union of all personalities, however distant from one another in time or space, in one great self-consciousness of the human family, and so again to re-act on each personality. While any generation or individual makes mankind's knowledge and experience his own, he unites himself with all the personalities of the past. While he lives and co-operates with the generation in which he lives, he makes its knowledge and experience his own, and unites himself with all the personalities of his age. So the work of perpetual re-union of all personalities, of all ages, goes on continually, elevating the self-consciousness and moral principle of mankind and re-acting perpetually on each individual. As the self-consciousness of humanity in its totality is an attribute of the eternal Deity, so the personal self-consciousness, the personality, is a self-conscious idea in the Deity, hence immortal as such. This is the fundamental idea to a philosophy of history. The growth of the self-consciousness of mankind and the proportional growth of the individual are always and continually the final cause of creation and history. To establish the efficient causes which produced this final cause is the main work of a philosophy of history.

So man's relations to God and nature as an active, free moral agent are clear. He is capacitated and prompted by natural impulses to co-operate with the Deity in bringing about the triumphs of mind over matter, of the conscious over the unconscious, in the steady progressions of mankind's self-consciousness, morality and freedom, and its reaction on the individual personalities, by which man and mankind are elevated to immortality, i. e., to an attribute and self-conscious idea in the Deity. The perpetual re-union of all personalities in the self-consciousness, and the progresses of science, art, philosophy, morals, freedom and religion in each generation, are the means to the end of nature's first cause becoming itself again in man's self-consciousness. This is the foundation of all philosophical ethics. Man's happiness depends on the triumphs of mind over matter.

The circle is closed and so is the cycle of my lectures for this season. Matter, force, law, God, creation, nature, man, history, will, intellect, self-consciousness, efficient, and final causes, aim, object, duty and destiny are clear conceptions, well defined ideas to us. We have solved the problems by the light of induction. The system is a complete organism, as far as induction leads, and beyond it I can not go in these lectures.

And now Ladies and Gentlemen permit me to speak a parting word to you. Twenty-two evenings we have met here in intellectual communion. Many a countenance I had not seen before, has become to me familiar and endeared. Search after the sacred gems of truth has united us in bonds of sacred friendship. I thank you all for the kind attention you have paid to my humble efforts. I thank you for your company on the rugged path of philosophical inquiry, for the sympathy you have manifested for my darling child, whose name is light, more light.

None will ever learn, under what painful and truly distressing influences these lectures were conceived, written and delivered. Many a time did I argue before you the most difficult problems, while my heart was aching, throbbing, weeping, almost breaking. The woeful passions and struggles of my soul were artificially hidden under the thick veil of arguments. None will ever learn, and learning it would never believe it, and yet I must tell it as a lesson for many, what I have done in the darkest hours of my existence, and how I have accomplished it.

Know it all, young people especially. When I was young, I chose a bride, the fairest of all maidens, and to her I made the sacred vow of fidelity. She always loved, cherished, encouraged and inspired me with confidence, boldness and fortitude. In the hours of success and victory she triumphed loudly over my gladness; in all trials, when earthly joys and mundane happiness deserted me, friends forsook me, and foes scorned, she was my angel of consolation, doubled and trebled her tenderness, and lavished it profusely on her hapless consort. Often have I abandoned her, roamed thoughtlessly far, far away, until I fell in the wild chase wounded, crushed, bleeding, moaning. Then I always returned home to her, and she always smiled again in holy sympathy, fanned cooling air at my glowing brows, kissed the grief from my forehead, wiped away the tears, balmed the wounds, and restored me to health and vigor. Eternally young, bright, kind, forbearing, affectionate and mild, she always was the same angel of consolation.

Again in the days of my sorrow, in affliction and distress, I have sought her and found her again. Again she has taken me by the hand and taught me the great principle, a man must be stronger than his grief. This immortal bride, this matchless angel, friends, is—SCIENCE, PHILOSOPHY, the eternal banner bearer of eternal truth. She never deserted, never deceived, never refused me her love and her consolation. The earnest disciple of science, philosophy, finds in the luminous regions of intelligence a world of happiness, also in the midst of seas of affliction and distress. One Eureka! at a discovered truth outweighs years of patience, anxiety and suffering; and each Eureka! is a diadem of glory from yonder heavenborn queen. Each Eureka! invigorates with self-consciousness, pride, force, happiness and glory in the mind's self-created paradise.

I recommend my bride to all, and promise them never to be jealous; for her heart is vast enough to embrace all, to love all, and to bless all.

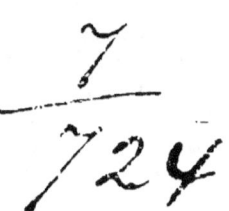

www.ingramcontent.com/pod-product-compliance
Lightning Source LLC
Chambersburg PA
CBHW020255170426
43202CB00008B/383